Praise for *The 21 Divisio*

"Based on his own deep insights as a *brujo* (wizard), Hector Salva has written a concise, colorful introduction to the divinities and rituals of Dominican Vodou. This is religious ethnography as it should be written and read."

> —**Donald Cosentino,** professor emeritus of world
> arts and cultures at the University of California,
> Los Angeles, and author of *Sacred Arts of Haitian Vodou*
> and *In Extremis: Death and Life in Twenty-First Century*
> *Haitian Art*

"As both an academic and a priest of Afro-Diasporic traditions, I often react with hopeful trepidation when anyone who doesn't wear both those hats publishes a book on the subject. I am therefore pleased with this offering from Hector Salva. Neither a dry analysis nor simply another attempt at a DIY manual, this book combines a personal journey of religious exploration with a broad view of the diverse and multifaceted tradition of Dominican Vodú (21 Divisions). Anyone reading this will come away with a better understanding of Afro-Dominican religiosity."

> —**Eoghan Craig Ballard**, PhD, ethnographer

"This book is a must-have! Papa Hector has filled it full of information needed to understand the Mysteries. *The 21 Divisions* contains valuable information for both the novice and the experienced worker. Papa Hector explains each division in detail that is easy to understand, and there are some hidden jewels, if you really listen. To be honest, when I was reading *The 21 Divisions,* I had to force myself to put it down. I have not read a book in a long time that held me captive like this one has. Papa Hector has written this book in a way that you feel like he is speaking directly to you. I cannot recommend this book enough!"

> —**Starr Casas**, author of *Old Style Conjure* and
> *Divination Conjure Style*

"From the riveting accounts of the hardships endured by the African slaves and their ingenious tactics for preserving their spiritual beliefs to a detailed description of Dominican Voodoo and its deities, *The 21 Divisions* is a masterpiece—a fascinating and reader-friendly explanation of these previously enigmatic magico-religious practices. Both my blood relatives and spiritual elders, all born in the early 1900s, practiced Cuban Santeria—

an African Traditional Religion (ATR) that closely parallels many aspects of Dominican Voodoo. Until I read *The 21 Divisions,* it was my fear that the moral codes of honor associated with those practices had died along with that generation. Instead, Hector Salva has emphatically preserved the integrity and outstanding character brought forth by the African slaves and deemed necessary to be an expert and honorable practitioner. This book is an exceptional, one-of-a-kind classic!"

—**Miss Aida**, author of *Hoodoo Cleansing*
and Protection Magic

"French and Spanish colonizers carved an island in half, but they could not kill its people's spirits. Many have heard of the African Diaspora traditions of the Haitian side of this island, but not as many know about the Dominican side. Papa Hector Salva introduces us to the world of the 21 Divisions of Dominican Voodoo. *The 21 Divisions* is a deep, colorful narrative about a lesser-known tradition and its continued survival inside the Dominican Republic and throughout the rest of the world. Papa Hector's contribution to our understanding of the Misterios and their servants is important and deeply needed."

—**Mambo Chita Tann**, author of *Haitian Vodou:*
An Introduction to Haiti's Indigenous Spiritual Tradition

"The 21 Divisions (Dominican Vodou) possesses a long and very complex oral tradition that resists losing its own essence. In his book *The 21 Divisions,* Hector Salva takes on the rigorous task (and personal challenge) of writing down these traditions and "secrets," and polishing them with great and remarkable precision, so that they are linguistically understandable to the public. The author approaches these oral traditions from a clearer and more modern point of view, writing with immense and delicate detail to deliver a complete manual of knowledge and anecdotes, and leading you to feel as if you are witnessing those wonderful passage rituals in the company of the spirits. Hector explains the workings of the *brujo's* magic, los Misterios, the spirits, and the Divisions in an amazing book about magic and *brujería.* It should be noted that the author's descriptive ability is brilliant. Far from being just another book full of infinite formulas, Hector focuses on providing a manual fully loaded with detailed information and knowledge properly explained, so that this guide becomes one of those books that you will consult again and again."

—**Elhoim Leafar**, author of *The Magical Art*
of Crafting Charm Bags

THE
21 DIVISIONS

THE
21 DIVISIONS

Mysteries and Magic of
DOMINICAN VOODOO

HECTOR SALVA

foreword by Hoodoo Sen Moise, author of *Working Conjure*

WEISER BOOKS

This edition first published in 2020 by Weiser Books, an imprint of
Red Wheel/Weiser, LLC
With offices at:
65 Parker Street, Suite 7
Newburyport, MA 01950
www.redwheelweiser.com

ISBN: 978-1-57863-681-5
Library of Congress Cataloging-in-Publication Data
available upon request

Cover design by Kathryn Sky-Peck
Cover illustration: "The Altar" by Lucia Mendez
Interior photos/images by Steve Amarillo / Urban Dessign LLC
Typeset in ITC Stone Serif and IM Fell

Printed in the United States of America
IBI
10 9 8 7 6 5 4 3 2 1

To the Absolute God and Divine Mysteries,
All People, My Teachers, Guides, Ancestors,
Family, Friends, Supporters and Readers . . .
May You Find Unity with the Absolute

Contents

What You Seek is Seeking You.

—Rumi

To the 21 Divisiones
Metresa MamboAnaisa Danto Pye Basico
And all those who have supported
and sacrificed for the Great Work—
"In Unity, There Is Power."

Foreword

The tradition of the 21 Divisions is one that holds many mysteries. The spirits of this wonderful tradition are there to bring guidance, assistance, freedom, healing, and so much more. And yet, they are often misunderstood and misinterpreted to mean something that is, in actuality, the complete opposite of the principles and teachings of this spiritual path.

One of the things I love about Hector Salva's book is the detailed explanations of the spirits served and the relationships that are developed. The Mysteries hold within them the power to create magical change and the wisdom to open doors that you never thought possible. From the bonds that hold us to the freedom we can achieve, service and relationships with the spirits are key. It is by that relationship, after all, that we tap into the magical force of the Mysteries and potency of change in all conditions. Hector goes into detail with the principles which guide and allow for the reader to experience, not just the words but also the power to grow.

The 21 Divisions has within it the potency of the world of the spirit that meets with the world of the physical: the principle of the crossroads itself. The relationships you develop with the spirits of the 21 Divisions continue to grow in love, strength, and wisdom, which in and of themselves are worth their weight in gold.

Hector Salva has done an absolutely beautiful job in explaining this magical and spiritual tradition so that both someone who knows very little as well as someone who knows very much will not only receive edification but also a real and true understanding.

The pages of this work are filled with knowledge, magic, and information that will surely be read and reread again and again. Whether you are a seasoned practitioner or a curious soul, you will find this text to be a great help in understanding a tradition that is literally dripping with magic.

I have known Hector for many years, and he is a priest who has always and without question been dedicated to the service of the spirits and the work of the Mysteries. He and I have been in many ceremonies together, serving the spirits, and I can tell you that there is a precision and knowledge that he exudes which has been inspirational to so many. As my godbrother in the Vodou, I have myself often sought his counsel on many things. He always advises with wisdom and speaks from a place of sheer dedication. This is one of the reasons he is who he is. As I sit here and write this, I am grateful for the wisdom I have received and the power of the spirits I have experienced and continue to.

Hector Salva has been a unique and ever-amazing presence in my own life, and that experience has been translated into the pages of this wonderful book. The edification you will receive from these pages will only continue to bring growth and wisdom to your own spiritual journey.

This book is one that no student of the Mysteries should be without. There is power in words, and the words on these pages are no exception. Hector Salva knows magic and he knows tradition, so let the power of his words bring understanding, magical change, and tremendous blessing in the life of every reader. You will not be disappointed.

—Hoodoo Sen Moise, author of *Working Conjure*

Introduction

The room was stuffy and hot, dozens of people had crowded themselves into a one-car garage. And yet, even with all of these people here, the room was silent except for Vincente, high priest of the 21 Divisions, hosting this event and sitting front and center while praying the Catholic sacraments. His voice fast and firm as sweat accumulated on his brow, his fingers counted the beads of a rosary he held in one hand as he rang a small silver bell in the other.

Before them was the altar composed of three shelves—the first two higher up on the wall and a third longer shelf that extended almost like a desk and waist-high, adorned with a multitude of saints and burning candles. Cigars, liquor, flowers, and various other liquids in bottles of all shapes and sizes were scattered amid the glowing lights. A beautiful wooden cross featured in the center, with two smaller crosses on either side. Another rosary of shiny red beads sat strewn on the altar. Various gifts, from jewelry and perfume to cash, fruit, and more liquor—brought by participants—sat on another table before the altar.

Having completed a lengthy litany of prayers, Vincente rose from his seat as some music started to play. More than a dozen people circled around him waving flags—large squares of satin fabrics in many vibrant colors attached to a tree branch the length of one's forearm—dancing and swaying to the music. Others started dancing here and there throughout the room, while some simply stood in silence watching the action.

Various individuals stepped into the circle to dance with Vincente. They would dance together for a little and then recede back into the crowd as another would come to dance. During the dance Vincente and his partner would twirl in small circles in opposite directions from time to time, then both dancing toward each other and then both slightly dancing backward. As the songs changed or when someone was really feeling the energy, random exclamations of *"Gracias a La Misericordia,"* or "Thanks to the grace of God," would be heard around the room.

This was the beginning of Vincente's ceremony to honor the 21 Divisions and call upon them to come *trabajar*—or work magic, consult, heal, and prophesize—for the congregation. Las 21 Divisiones, or the 21 Divisions, are a group of elevated and Divine Beings known as Misterios, created by God to serve God and help humanity. The 21 Divisions is also the name of the tradition, which many adherents don't consider a religion but rather a spiritual practice that goes hand in hand with their religious views. The Tradition of Las 21 Divisiones is also called Dominican Voodoo. In some locales, it's also known as Los Misterios, meaning "The Mysteries"—the same word used to collectively talk about these spirits.

The 21 Divisions is a form of Catholic Afro-Caribbean shamanism. It combines elements of the Native Caribbean religious traditions of the Tainos, African shamanism, Roman Catholicism, Haitian Vodou, and European magic and occultism. However, the three strongest elements of the 21 Divisions come from the religions of the native Tainos and Arawaks who originally inhabited the Caribbean, the Africans who were brought as slaves to Hispaniola (now, Haiti and the Dominican Republic), and the Catholic religion of the Spaniards. It's a unique blend of beliefs and practices from these major cultures that form its foundation.

An Oral Tradition

This path is and was transmitted through oral teachings. Handed down orally and at first within the bloodlines of the family only, the many ways of practicing are not recorded in any book. This leads to great changes in short periods of time, as anyone who has ever played a game of telephone or whisper down the lane is well aware of. The tradition is also dependent upon human memory, the capacity and willingness to learn and absorb information, and the commitment of the students so that they can be fit enough to pass the teachings on. After receiving the teachings, the student-turned-teacher must also be able to correctly and fully share them with others.

In order to preserve the tradition and its practices, priests and priestesses came together creating secret groups to hand down the secrets, knowledge, and rituals. Families who had preserved the knowledge within them did the same. Rules and manner of practice, as well as other information would be shared and passed down to apprentices and students. Through various rituals, individuals would be admitted into the secret group and become a part of it, thus establishing lineages—lines of people deriving from the original group who continue its teachings and practices.

As such, there are regional variances throughout the country. So the names of the groups and how the Misterios are placed together vary from region to region, lineage to lineage, and so on. In some locales they split the Divisions according to elements or tribes. Others divide by the sense of the types of Misterios and where they focus their labor. In some areas, some Divisions are recognized, and in other areas, they are unknown or little known. Regionally as well, various Misterios or Divisions hold different levels of importance. Some practices are influenced more by Haitian culture, others are more Catholic, and yet others feel the heritage of the Taino Indians.

This is part of the difficulty in writing a book about this or any other oral tradition. What may be true in one place may not be true in another. This is the path of the Misterios for a reason. Only by taking your *own* journey on the spiritual path will you begin to be illumined as to the Sacred Truth. The Mysteries can be unraveled and understood but only through walking the path properly. For as we always say, many are called, but few are chosen. Still, each lineage works and is correct because each is a complete system, a microcosm of the macrocosm. So as long as the practitioner is delving only into the practices of the lineage to which he or she corresponds and not mixing them, the practitioner will reach the goals and, with persistence, the answer to the Great Mystery. At this center is the Great Truth—the truth upon which all paths ultimately must agree.

However, as with many oral traditions, you'll find that you'll always have someone claiming something different. Now this is okay, because of the tradition's variances. But no matter where it is found, certain spiritual laws govern all practices. It is these laws that truly determine the rightness or wrongness of a given practice. Like all things, there is a proper framework that keeps it all together and flowing. Some individuals, as in all walks of life, are confused and like to confuse others. This is simply due to ignorance and how a lack of knowledge snowballs upon itself. Unfortunately, a fool is often someone who doesn't even know that they don't know, and there are many fools. A true master, having unlocked the Mystery, will be able to recognize truth and falsehood wherever he goes.

I've written this book according to my own lineage: the Lineage of the San Elias, Baron of the Cemetery. This is one of the oldest lineages of the 21 Divisions, as Baron was one of the first Misterios to become established in the New World. This lineage established the Cofradia, or Brotherhood, of San Elias in Santiago, Dominican Republic. As such, the teachings and information presented to you here are based on my lineage and experiences as a priest and participant of this beautiful tradition.

The 21 Divisions Beliefs and Foundation

God and His Mysteries

According to the 21 Divisions, there is one God known as Papa Dios or Papa Bondye. *Papa Dios* means "Father God" in Spanish. *Papa Bondye* refers to *Bon*, "good" in French and Kreyol, and *Dye*, "God" in same languages—meaning "Good God," as in God the Father. God created the universe and everything within it. God also created Universal Laws. Early on in his creation, he made Divine Beings known as the Misterios or Mysteries. Once he completed creating and setting everything into place, he turned over the management of his creation to the Misterios. However, God is immanent, which means that the Divine is manifested through and sustains the material world. Therefore, God manifests God's will through the actions of the Misterios. God is also seen in the Catholic Holy Trinity—Father, Son, and Holy Spirit, three and yet one.

Not all Misterios are good and work for God. As in Christian theology, a group of these angels followed the commands of Lucifer, fell from grace, and became demons. Working to defeat humanity and on the behalf of evil, they guide people toward selfishness, greed, and all the other evils that exist. Thus, a battle between good and evil exists in which one's soul as well as one's life is constantly being influenced and affected by contradictory influences. To many *servidores* this corresponds to the Misterios de La Luz, the angels of light who remained with God, and the Misterio Malos or Oscuros, the bad angels or Misterios of Darkness. The first work on God's behalf to improve humanity. The second are often known to be called *djab*, *baka*, and *demonios*. *Djab* and *demonio* both mean "demon." However, the word *djab* also can refer to an enraged Mystery, even if it works under God.

The 21 Divisions are made up of all the Misterios of Light that work in God's behalf. Those that serve and practice the 21 Divisions also work on behalf of the spirits that are under God's patronage. These Misterios act as agents of the Divine, enacting and expressing God's Will. God created the Misterios to help guide man toward God and the good. As such, they also uphold the Universal Laws. As emissaries of God, they can be interacted with and communicate the Divine plan.

The Divine Beings known as Misterios are much like the angels and saints of Catholicism in that each Misterio has a realm or domain over which he or she exerts power and influence. Each has sacred days, colors, and associations. Each one has his likes, dislikes, character, and personality. Male Misterios are known as *Lwa* or *Lwases* and females as *Metresas*. However, when speaking of them as a mixed group they are referred to as Lwa or Misterios.

The Misterios are also referred to as *santos* or saints. Most are also connected to and represented by a Catholic saint, but this doesn't mean that practitioners confuse them for the saints themselves. The names of the Misterios and their identities are not the same as the saint they are represented by. The Misterios are, in fact, the gods and spirits of the African and Taino traditions of those enslaved by the Catholic Spaniards. In order to keep their religions and beliefs, the slaves adopted and integrated the beliefs and practices of their oppressors with their own traditions. Due to the religious and socioeconomic environment of the Dominican Republic, the degree of influence of Catholicism in the 21 Divisions is quite strong.

Also as with the saints of Catholicism, a person can potentially be elevated to the status of a Misterio. Some of the Misterios were actual living people who were deified after death by their people. So there are historical figures, actual people, who by having made many miracles have become Misterios. By receiving service and devotees, helping people, and creating more and more miracles, a spirit of a person or other being can over time gain the necessary light—just like a saint—to literally transform into a being of light.

The 21 Divisions

The Misterios are divided into groups known as *Divisiones* or *Divisions*. Each group contains an array of spirits with an energy that binds them together. There are said to be twenty-one groups, thus the name 21 Divisions. Beginning at the highest level, there are three major divisions: the Black Division, the White Division, and the Blue Division. The Black Division encompasses the two major divisions of earth and fire. The White Division is also known as the Rada Division and connected to the energy of air. The Blue Division is of water and encompasses the Misterios of the Taino Indians of the islands and the water spirits. Each of these three major divisions is split into seven divisions each. Thus, we get a total of 21 Divisions. Furthermore, there are magical meanings, sacredness, and associations in the numbers 3, 7, and 21. All are considered lucky and holy numbers.

These numbers are symbolic, though, because in reality, the divisions number more than 21, even if most practitioners do not work with all of them individually. Some state that the 21 Divisions are the gods of the twenty-one tribes that came to Santo Domingo from Africa. However, more than twenty-one different tribes of African slaves came to the Americas and also ended up in Santo Domingo. The 21 Divisions is rather a creolized mix of many spirits, both from Africa as well as the Americas, specifically Hispaniola. There are many divisions that are named after African tribes, so it's easy to understand the conclusion; however, often even those divisions contain other Misterios that have no origin in Africa or are now creolized.

As far as a final number, the Misterios are in the end innumerable. One practitioner I know says there are 121 Misterios in total, yet others say there are thousands. In practice, most individuals only work with a few of the divisions and, even within that context, only a few spirits in totality. Even the priests and priestesses will only work with a core group of the Misterios, but will be responsible to do certain rituals to care for them all. A priest will also work with various Misterios when needed and directed to do so. The truth is that no one could or even should serve all of the Misterios. This is well known by those who are trained.

Two Worlds in One

The room and the music were infectious; the energy roaring from Vincente's ceremony was in full swing. People danced with vigor and delight. Others laughed and socialized. Vincente and a small group of individuals, however, were totally in the world of the dance and singing the sacred songs.

Eventually Vincente's body started to convulse lightly, like a leaf rustling in a warm, soft spring breeze. His arms shook vigorously as he lifted them up and down, followed by a deep wailing moan. People around him gently supported his body, making sure he wouldn't fall yet also not disturbing the proceedings. As this happened, a large heavy-set woman with light brown eyes and chocolate skin came forward with a white bedsheet and a pink kerchief. As he continued to gently shake and shiver, crying profusely, she, along with a few other women, stretched the sheet out over the floor. He was then guided to stand upon it. His face softened as a pink kerchief was tied around his head.

Vincente was no more. Although his body was present, his spirit, soul, and consciousness were not. They were elsewhere. Instead his body was being occupied and used by a Divine Being known as Metresili, the Spirit of Love and Abundance. While she occupied his body, the people present would and could interact directly with the Divine Love and understand its messages to them.

A white enamel basin filled with water strewn with flowers was brought before her to wash her hands. A fancy pink bottle of perfume with an atomizer was brought to her. She sprayed copious amounts of perfume over herself and the space around her while tears gently rolled down the sides of her face. The room had again gone completely silent and still. Her voice came forward just a bit louder than a whisper:

"I've come to take the sorrows away from my children. . . . The waves have crashed upon the shores and they (the shores) haven't kept well. Wherever there is stone the sea will continue to beat upon it, who do you think will win? The stone or the water? It's not the fault of the sea but of the shores. . . ."

Various individuals came forward to receive her blessings—her children, I presumed. She whispered in each of their ears after having "shaken hands," with each person. Shaking hands with her consisted of interlacing one's pinky fingers with hers and moving the hands, crossing each other back and forth. One person's face lit up as a wave of relief came over her; a stream of tears of joy came down her face with giggles. Metresili sent various thank-you messages to people present by telling her children to pass them along. While this was going on a champagne glass filled with bright red soda pop was brought for her to sip.

After concluding what she wanted to say, she gently waved goodbye as tears began flowing down her face again. Vincente's body went limp into the arms of the same woman who had laid out the sheet for Metresili to stand on. This was Lila, Vincente's assistant, I would later come to learn. His body was guided over to a chair to recover. After a few moments, his eyes sprang open, and Vincente was completely back in his body.

Metresili would be one of many Misterios who would take over Vincente's body and the bodies of various other participants that night. They were being called upon and honored in this ceremony. In return, the people sought blessings, healings, answers to their questions, and solutions to their problems. They would look to the Misterios to aid them in fixing that which nothing else could. Only by Divine intervention and assistance from the Other world would they find what they needed. Some sought love, others protection, while yet others needed healing or to get some loved one out of jail. Their needs were many, but they knew the incredible power of the Misterios, where miracles are not rare, but common and even the wildest things can happen.

In the 21 Divisions, the spiritual world and the physical world are intrinsically linked. Actions taken in either realm affect all others. Like a stone being tossed in a pond, what we do has ripples in our lives and the lives of others. As such, each side needs the other. The Spirits need people just as much as people need the Spirits. One cannot exist without the other. Therefore, there are rituals and ceremonies that can bring the physical and spiritual worlds into direct contact. Through these rituals, such as Vincente's above, the Misterios can manifest and communicate prophecies, Divine messages to assist the living, create miracles, work healing, and help those that serve them.

The Misterios communicate many different ways. Through dreams, signs, and synchronicity is one way they often convey messages to those who serve them. They also use visions, spiritual sight, voices, and other spiritual gifts and abilities that have been developed by their servants. However, the most common way for a Misterio to come through, communicate, work, and heal is the vehicle of trance possession. The person is said to be *montao*, or mounted by the Misterio.

This is one of the most defining factors within Dominican Voodoo. The focus is almost always the induction of trance in one form or another in most rituals. Dominican Voodooists are specialists in this capacity and amazing at it. In most lineages, one cannot be a full-fledged priest without this capacity. The purpose of mounting is direct communication, experience, and channeling to the Divine and the Power.

During possession, the individuals mounted by the Misterios are known as *horses* or *Caballos de Misterios*. The caballo loses consciousness, temporarily having the soul leave the body, though they are still connected. The Misterios take over the body by using it as a vessel or a horse. Since they are taking the full ownership (possession) of the head, brain, and consciousness, they are said to have mounted the person and be riding the horse. Once they have fully mounted their horse, the Misterios proceed to do whatever they came to do. While they are mounted, the characteristics and appearance of that person change to that of the Misterio who has taken over the body.

Once the Misterio is present, the people will address and interact with the Misterio and not the person whose body is occupied. For example, if a female spirit takes over a male body, the people will address the spirit by her name, call it a she, and expect her behaviors and characteristics. It is she who is there, her spirit, and not the soul of the individual's body she is using. The Misterio will be given his or her things and then will begin to interact with the people present. Each Misterio has certain items that they use while they mount a horse.

While the person is mounted by the Misterio, that individual will have no memory of the events that took place. Only once the Misterio has left will the soul of the person come back to take possession of the body. Once back, the individual will be exhausted and worn down from the experience. The Misterios run an incredible amount of energy through the horse's body. It is like 220 volts going through a 110-volt channel.

Servants of the Mysteries

Everyone is born with a Guardian Misterio. This Misterio is assigned to you by God, like your guardian angel, and is meant to guide, protect, and help you. Likewise each individual is born with a certain amount of spiritual power (*fuerza*), which varies from person to person. It is this power that determines the degree or level of connection to and awareness of the spiritual world. Some individuals are born with such power and connection that they are able to communicate and have a relationship with the Misterios.

The path of the 21 Divisions is initiatory/apprenticeship-oriented and has a hierarchical structure. In other words, on the Dominican Voodoo path, one has a spiritual teacher, guide, and parent, who is known as a *Madrina/Mama* (female) or *Padrino/Papa* (male). There are levels of initiation and processes of apprenticeship that happen to develop fuerza and connection to it.

A believer and follower of the Misterios is known as a *devoto*, or devotee. This is a person who believes and follows the Misterios, but without the ability to work with the Misterios or have open communication with them. The Misterios protect and bless their devotos, interceding and helping them when there are issues. A devoto, however, will have a *brujo*, or priest, to go to in order to receive the guidance of the Misterios.

A practitioner of the 21 Divisions is known as a *servidor de Misterio*, a servant of the Mystery. Females are known as *servidoras*. First and foremost, the person is servant to the Greatest Mystery, God, and after God, his Divine Mysteries of Light, the Misterios of the 21 Divisions. Through his connection to the spiritual world and serving the Misterios, the servant comes closer to God and the Lwases, which brings blessings, protection, health, and good luck. Aside from these worldly goals, a practitioner will also be able to develop spiritual gifts, powers, and abilities, attaining greater and greater spiritual progress.

Servidores who have the fuerza and illuminated connection are able to work with the Misterios to varying degrees. However, most servidores' powers are limited usually to him- or herself and the closest loved ones. Their spirituality and spiritual powers are for their own benefit and to improve their own lives. Such servidores may or may not be initiated. However, initiation develops the servidores' spiritual gifts and abilities, as well as giving them greater connection to their Misterios. Either way, they will always have a Padrino or brujo from whom they receive guidance and help when it comes to their spiritual path.

A brujo (male) or bruja (female) is a priest of the 21 Divisions. He or she can affect the physical world, their own life, and the lives of others through various offerings, rituals, and ceremonies, which are often called *services* or *servicios*. For simplicity's sake, I will use *brujo* overall in our discussions. He has *Misterios para Trabajar* or *Mysteries for Working* for others. By working with the Misterios, a brujo can be a vehicle for Divine healing, help, and guidance to themselves and others. The brujo dedicates himself to the development of his spiritual power and connection with the Misterios. Thus he is able to work and manipulate the power in order to make miracles. Magic is a central element of the practice and can be used to attract luck, love, success, and many of one's goals and aims.

An initiated brujo of Dominican Voodoo is known as a *Papa Boko*. An initiated bruja is a *Mama Mambo*. They have received the secret rituals and wisdom that have been passed down through the centuries in a sacred lineage from master brujos to students. Not all brujos undergo initiation.

Ceremonies and Rituals

The main public ceremonies of a brujo are the *Mani*, the *Priye/ Prille*, the *Hora Santa*, and *Fiesta de Palos*. They can be carried out for many reasons, such as to petition or to make payment to or thank a Lwa or group of Misterios. These ceremonies are also given on behalf of clients, apprentices, or initiates.

The Priye/Prilli and Hora Santa ceremonies are special prayer ceremonies for the Misterios. The Hora Santa is more Catholic in form and format. The Prilli usually focuses on singing songs, known as *salves*, to the Misterios. During these ceremonies, the Misterios come and confer messages and guidance. The Mani, a very similar ceremony, is done with the addition of certain key offerings given to the Lwases, and may also have a Fiesta de Palos given.

The Fiesta de Palos or Fiesta de Atabales is often held on the feast day of the Misterio who is being celebrated. It can be held after the processions of the Cofradias as a part of that celebration. It can also be held on its own. The ceremony focuses on the music produced by three large drums, known as Palo drums because they used to be made from the trunk of a large tree (*palo*). The Palo drums are consecrated and sacred to the spirits, holding the power to call them forward. The Fiesta de Palos is no small undertaking, as it is a huge ceremony where dancing and possession are the centerpieces.

Some brujos don't host large feasts and ceremonies and work without any society. Many brujos don't initiate or accept apprentices either. In this case, the brujo usually honors his Misterios with the same rituals but only with those in his inner circle. Sometimes he may belong to a Cofradia or Hermandad to fulfill this for himself. Very commonly, he goes to his own initiator, or Papa Boko, to help him take care of such needs. At other times, he may hire or collaborate with another brujo to hold large ceremonies when required by the Misterios.

Temples and Structures

Unlike many other religions and spiritual traditions, the 21 Divisions doesn't center its practice around a temple. As you will come to see, this came about because of the legality of practicing the traditions throughout its history. In Dominican Voodoo, the *sosyete*, or society, is what is considered the temple—the people, the congregation under the brujo's care. It is not a physical structure. This society is very loosely organized. It will consist of usually the brujos; his assistants, initiates, and apprentices; and his clients. The only time that the society usually comes together is when the brujo has a large ceremony such as a Prille or Mani to hold. Most of the time the brujo works with people one-on-one. As such, the brujo is most prominently a for-hire magician, healer, and shaman.

Animal Sacrifice in Dominican Voodoo

Let's discuss animal sacrifice with regard to Dominican Voodoo. Again, this is another subject of controversy even among practitioners. Some lineages of Dominican Voodoo sacrifice animals and others don't. One isn't better or worse, stronger or weaker; they are simply not the same. It's more common to see animal sacrifice in lineages with greater Haitian Vodou influence. Spiritual practices near the borderlands with Haiti therefore more often conduct things in this manner. However, in many lineages, it's considered to be connected with black magic, demons, and evil Misterios. In those lines, animal sacrifice is not practiced at all. Some lines only sacrifice animals during initiations.

In any case, animal sacrifice is not that common in practice. Even in lines where it is done, it's reserved for only initiations and extremely severe cases and circumstances. Only priests of those lineages who have received the proper training and permission to carry out animal sacrifice are allowed to do so. In the country areas, where it's common to butcher a large animal when feeding a huge group of people, brujos will commonly sacrifice the animal to the Misterios by killing the animal in a consecrated way and then using it for both feeding the people and the Misterios. However, it's not something you'll likely see that often.

Understand the Roots,
Know the Tree:
History of 21 Divisions

In order to truly understand the 21 Divisions, you will need to know the history of the people and the island on which it came forth. The Dominican Republic, birthplace of the traditions of the 21 Divisions, is located on the island of Hispaniola. The island is divided into two countries: Haiti, which owns the western half, and the Dominican Republic, which owns the eastern half. The capital of the Dominican Republic is Santo Domingo, which was the first official Spanish colony in what was "discovered by Columbus" and is known as the "New World."

The truth is that the island was already inhabited by the native Taino, who would, in time, be enslaved and eradicated by Columbus and other Europeans. Before the Taino population was so extremely decimated, however, Europeans brought African slaves to Santo Domingo and other areas of the Dominican Republic. There they worked the African and Indian slaves in their fields and farms. In addition, Spanish settlers had children with their slaves. These children and their descendants would be what are now known as the Dominican people. The primary language of the Dominican Republic is Spanish.

Now, the Spanish that came to the island were Catholic, and they were very staunch in their beliefs. The Spanish Catholics were very serious about converting the slaves under Spanish rule. In fact, many of the first slaves brought to and kept in the Spanish colony had already been slaves in Spain and were forced to convert to Catholicism there. However, as their demands increased, they didn't have the same amount of time to route workers to Spain and convert them. They started bringing slaves directly over from Africa. The Spanish, in essence, worked really hard to erase the Indian and African culture and identity from their slaves. Over time they succeeded in many ways—but not all.

The Africans and the Indians also had their very own strong beliefs. They were loyal to their gods, spirits, and beliefs, and many would die for them. However, they were also creative. They hid their religious beliefs and practices and used the same Catholic religion they were being forced to adopt to help them preserve and save their ancestral ways. They passed their practices on to their children and grandchildren, keeping the religion alive in their hearts, spirits, and bodies. Many of the slaves that would end up in the DR would be of West African origin, and thus these slaves served gods known as Vodoun. The Indian gods and spirits were also preserved in this way, and practices of European magic and witchcraft came from the Spanish as well. All of these would blend together to become what is now known as the 21 Divisions.

Now the slaves came from all over Africa, but slaves of certain tribes outnumbered other tribes to varying degrees on various parts of the island. Likewise, the influence of the natives varied all over the island since there were so few left. The first type of Voodoo that started to form on the island is known as the Tcha Tcha lineage. This is the Lineage of the 21 Divisions and Dominican Voodoo. The tradition was passed down orally and in secret. Naturally, it varied from region to region, place to place, as it was now a mix of the beliefs, spirits, and gods of so many people who had come together.

Very real risks came from practicing the 21 Divisions or Voodoo openly in the old times, which in fact were not that long ago. People who did so risked imprisonment, fines, or even death. Many died for practicing the tradition. Even today, discrimination against practitioners continues to exist and impact them. Therefore, the 21 Divisions are intertwined with Catholic ritual, liturgy, and practices, which have become intrinsic in the practice of caring for and serving the Misterios. The slaves used the saints to shelter the Misterios. Each Misterio became tied to a saint in order to continue to worship and serve the Misterios without being discovered. In the Dominican Republic, in particular, Catholicism was so strong that in order for the Misterios to survive they had to keep their masks closer and take them off less often.

This happened all over the islands in the Caribbean, the slaves making things work out in their circumstances in order to preserve their religions. In Haiti, this syncretizing would become known as Vodou or *Sevis Ginen*. This is the closest relative of Dominican Voodoo, and you'll see how they are connected. In Cuba, the African practices that would be preserved would become Lucumi, sometimes known as Santeria, and Palo Mayombe. In Trinidad and Tobago, the ancestral ways would become Shango Baptist. In Puerto Rico, Brujeria and Espiritismo would end up home for the practices remaining from the slaves and originating people.

The 21 Divisions are one of the spiritual traditions/religions of the Caribbean under the title Afro-Caribbean traditions. These traditions share many common beliefs and elements. The 21 Divisions make up one half of the Sanse tradition of Puerto Rico, which is a type of Puerto Rican shamanism. Out of all these practices, the 21 Divisions are the most Catholicized. At times it can be very, very difficult to differentiate the two. Although there are other sects of the traditions that hold more Indian, Haitian, or African influence, they are unto themselves.

While all of this was happening on the eastern side of the island, the western side had been taken over by the French. This side became Haiti. The French were less religious compared to the Spanish. They didn't work as hard to "make true converts" from the slaves they had or brought in. Rather they carried out a more minimal indoctrination process. However, like the Spanish, they did hand out grave punishments for those practicing "Voodoo." The slaves on the Haitian side, however, rose up and overthrew the French in the first successful slave revolt in history.

The Dominicans had a different history. Although they got rid of the Spanish in 1821, the traditions and religions of the slaves had already been wiped out to a greater degree. After the departure of the Spanish, they were invaded by Haiti and occupied for two decades. The Haitians brought their Voodoo and spiritual practices. In fact, some of it mixed with the 21 Divisions. The Dominicans eventually reclaimed their freedom from Haiti in a bloodless coup. So as you can see, the history and relationship between Haiti and the Dominican Republic have always been close and very much intertwined. The fact is that the dividing line between the two countries is a man-made border that has always been very porous. There has always been of bleeding of cultures, influences, and exchange between Haiti and the Dominican Republic—and this has not always been for the good. There have been much horror and bloodshed between the two countries. But there has also been the intermixing of blood and bloodlines and spiritual practices.

The Dominicans returned to Spanish rule to gain protection from Haiti. But that lasted only four years before they again got rid of the Spanish to become independent yet again.

Cofradia y Hermandades: The Survival of the Misterios

Catholicism provided the perfect veneer to safeguard ancestral indigenous and African spiritual practices. In the Dominican Republic, the way that the people came together to celebrate the Misterios and carry out group rituals was under the cover of a *Cofradia* or *Hermandad*. The Cofradias are social groups that all center themselves around upholding Catholic morals, supporting the community through acts of charity and goodness, and working for the social good. A Hermandad, which means "brotherhood," is often a smaller group of the same nature. In spite of the names both groups are coed.

Cofradias were established by and backed by the Catholic Church. The church also heavily encouraged the participation of all slaves as their way of working to convert slaves to the new religion. Although, technically Hermandades and Cofradias could be formed by any group of people, at first the Catholics only allowed white slave masters to do so. So there were and are Cofradias and Hermandades that are totally Catholic and not connected in any way to the 21 Divisions. Priests then decided it was important for the slaves to be given time to participate in the activities of the Cofradia. Likewise, the slaves were to not work on the feast days of the patron saints and were to be given time to socialize and spend together.

Quickly noticing how the slaves embrace the saints and their dedication, the priests decided that they should be allowed to open their own Cofradias. Many of the Catholic priests, happy to see the slaves participating, also slowly allowed for African practices to be brought in, thinking it would further encourage conversion. They felt it would be good for the slaves to incorporate a bit of their own culture and "make it theirs," so to speak. Unknowingly and unwittingly, they ended up helping preserve the Misterios, the very thing they worked so hard to eradicate. Convinced that the slaves were embracing the new religion of Catholicism, they didn't mind if they brought in a bit of their culture.

However, the way it worked in the Dominican Republic for the African slaves was that often either a family or a group of brujos would band together to form the Cofradia. The Cofradias therefore became the storehouse for the knowledge and traditions of the 21 Divisions. Many of these Cofradias were some of the first establishments of African spiritual practices in the Americas and continue to operate in various parts of the island.

A Cofradia required a group of at least nine individuals with each charged with a task. Cofradias were a highly organized structure as to their governing and activities. They all were dedicated to a specific saint and celebrated the feast of this patron annually. On these dates, a novena or velada was held in honor of the patron saint. A novena is a prayer process that takes place over nine consecutive days. During veladas, candle vigils were placed near the icon of the patron saint, and various members took turns "watching" the saint by staying up all night long and praying constantly until the ultimate time of the feast. On the feast day, the Cofradia went out with the Catholic church in a procession for the saint. The processions and celebrations of the Cofradias were always accompanied and followed by dances, African drumming, and music.

After all the Catholic rituals had been carried out, the slaves were allowed to relax and socialize. Not understanding the practices of the slaves, their oppressors simply saw them holding a social event while, in actuality, this is when the service to the Misterios would begin. Communal feasting was always also a central activity within this part of the events. The altar, initially set up in honor of the saint, was now laden with food offerings to the Misterios.

The music would encompass both the saints and the Misterios. The drums beat the rhythms of the African ancestors, particularly those of the Kongo, as the dances became the method through which the souls of the servants would ascend into heaven, leaving the body an empty vessel so that the Divine Misterios could descend within them. Now the rum, the sacred drinks, perfumes, and tobaccos could all come out and be employed in service to the Divine.

This is the way the 21 Divisions and the Misterios survived— all right under the eyes of the slave masters. Naturally due to the circumstances, many elements of rituals and ceremonies had to be altered and adapted. Tools used had to be minimal and things that could be utilized right out in the open. The servants of the 21 Divisions learned to perfect their capacity to allow the Misterios to possess them and be able to do great spiritual work with very little accoutrements. Due to the laws of those times, a white Dominican could go to a slave Cofradia's event but not vice versa. So the slaves had to be very careful about their activities. They could face an influx of outsiders at any time. What was Catholic and what was Voodoo had to become well enmeshed, undetectable. Many of the Misterios' Voodoo names and Catholic saints are now synonymous. Some Misterios with lesser followings have even lost their African names altogether and are only known by their Catholic counterparts.

Common Roots: 21 Divisions and Haitian Vodou

The Tcha Tcha lineage existed on both sides of the island before it was divided between the French and Spanish. Haitian Vodou and Dominican Voodoo thus share the same root. However, each practice evolved differently based on the different European influences. Each practice grew in the manner in which it could survive and thrive. Likewise, there were fewer Indians mixed into the blood on the French side, as by the time the French arrived there were fewer Indians overall. So each type of practice took on influences to varying degrees from the various tribes of the African slaves, Tainos, and Arawaks in the respective areas, alongside of the dominating culture of either French or Spanish. For example, the language of practice in Haiti became Kreyol and in the Dominican Republic Spanish.

Now, because each was evolving in different cultures under different circumstances, the Misterios adapted to the needs of their people and the capacities of the same as they always do. But the essence of the Misterios and the Mystery itself remained the same. You'll also see that they share many terms and words, although the way they define those terms and the connotations that they carry may be different. Practices are also shared among the two.

So what are the major differences?

As mentioned before, the French didn't stress conversion to Catholicism as much as the Spanish did. Furthermore, the Haitians were able to liberate themselves from the French much sooner, and a large percentage of the first enslaved Haitians were actually first-generation Africans. Out from under French rule, the Haitians were able to practice their Voodoo more freely. Thus, they were able to retain larger parts of their African cultures and beliefs.

Haitian Vodou retained many more of the aspects of the religions originating in Africa as well. Because its practitioners viewed it as a religion, the mindset and memory of the ancestral ways were more entrenched. Haitian Vodou includes Catholic rituals, but not to the same degree, and they are obviously much more of a veneer. In Haiti it is common for Vodou priests to operate in temples, and in some Haitian temples all Catholic elements have been removed or were never even incorporated.

Dominican Voodoo, on the other hand, became much more magical in orientation. Its value comes less from its religious aspect as from its practicality, the results of its magic, and its pragmatism. Dominican Vodouisants almost always consider themselves Catholics as far as their religion goes and the 21 Divisions as their spiritual practice. In the 21 Divisions, it is the altar room of the brujo that's the central ceremonial space. There are no temples. This altar room is usually a room in the priest's own house. While temples do exist, they are way less common.

Catholic rituals and ceremonies are also an integral part of the 21 Divisions and their magic. For many of the Dominican Misterios, the Catholic saint has become intrinsically connected to the Misterio and that never changes. In Haitian Vodou, it is not uncommon for the Misterios' Catholic counterparts to change from region to region or in fact from temple to temple.

Public and group rituals that were common in African and Indian practices and therefore were retained in the Haitian form of Voodoo are uncommon in the 21 Divisions. Also whereas the community is central to the Haitian Vodou priest, the brujo of the 21 Divisions most commonly works in private. Another area of difference is the music and drumming. The songs, the drum rhythms, and the dances between the two traditions have diverged.

The Dominican Republic: Trujillo and Anti-Haitianism

Unfortunately, Haiti and the Dominican Republic have been at odds since the territories were formed. This feud has yet to stop as of this writing. Many Haitians and Dominicans don't want to admit that we are invariably tied and intertwined with each other. There are many hurts on both sides. I'm not here to pick sides or judge right or wrong. I can only speak for what I've witnessed and experienced.

There were invasions back and forth, especially near the border. There was also a mixing of culture, spirituality, beliefs, practices, and bloodlines. As explained, in the 1800s the Haitians had invaded and many settled on the Dominican side. After the invasion was squelched, a lot of these folks stayed. But even after, the border was always very porous.

However, in 1930, a new president came into power in the Dominican Republic. And Rafael Trujillo Molina had a plan, which was to rid the Dominican Republic of the Haitians and also the mixed-blood Dominican Haitians. He started a campaign of Anti-Haitianism. He ordered a terrible massacre that led to the deaths of approximately 18,000 Haitians. He also took in huge populations of white refugee immigrants in an effort to "whiten" the population of the Dominican Republic. And so, the wars continue.

In the Dominican Republic, generally only very few wish to acknowledge the Haitian influences within their culture. Not surprisingly, most prefer to demonize and reject it. Many people with a Haitian ancestry or background will outright deny it. This is understandable considering history and the prejudices it has left behind. In some places there's strong virulent hatred between Haitians and Dominicans that can at times lead to death. To admit it can cause discrimination and unnecessary problems.

An example:

I was in Santo Domingo, capital of the Dominican Republic. I was having lunch at a beautiful little outdoor café in the middle of the city with a friend, Domingo, who is also a brujo. As we sat there, chatting away and enjoying the sun, a woman of about thirty came up to us to speak with Domingo. Domingo introduced us to each other and offered her a seat. Her name was Ada, and she was Domingo's neighbor who lived up the street from him. She sat down and we chatted for a little while. In the midst of this, I could see the Lwa behind her and the issues she was facing.

So I asked her "You are Haitian, right?"

"No, no, no. I am Dominican. Haitians . . . ugh," she responded quickly and firmly with a disgusted look on her face.

"So your parents aren't Haitian; your family isn't from Haiti?" I pressed.

"No, we are pure Dominican."

"Uh oh," I replied. *"Excuse'm, Cheri, m panse m te we moun pa'm"* (Excuse me, dear, I thought I found my people). I responded to her in Kreyol, knowing she was not being truthful.

Her eyes lit up and widened, filled with surprise. But she carried on with her denials: "What? Sorry, I didn't understand. I don't understand that."

"Okay," I said, leaving it at that.

After about ten more minutes of chatting with us she departed.

About half a week later, I got a call from Domingo. He was inviting me to her house, as she had invited him to come over and asked if I was still around to bring me along.

Once we got there, a little after three in the afternoon, she received and greeted us. We set up on the porch to have some wonderful espresso and smoke some cigarettes. After some initial talk, she said to me, "Why did you think I was Haitian?"

"You have the Misterios that are Haitian," I told her.

"So, you are a brujo like Domingo?" she responded, looking curious.

I nodded.

"And how do you speak Kreyol?"

"I thought you didn't understand . . . ," I responded with a smirk.

"Well, I *am* Haitian. My mother is Haitian, and my father is Dominican. But you know, around here, it is not good to be Haitian. People don't like you if you are Haitian, and they give you problems," she explained.

"I know and understand," I told her.

"That's why I told you no. But I have never met a Dominican who can actually speak Kreyol. No Dominican I know wants to be bothered with it; they say, 'Why would I care to learn the language of the Haitians?' You speak Kreyol better than me. I was born and raised here, so my Kreyol isn't strong, but my mother taught me it."

"I lived in Haiti, was initiated as a Houngan, and practice both the 21 Divisions and Vodou. . . ."

After that, Ada and I were fast friends. In time, she, her mother, and several of her other family members became my godchildren. In the 21 Divisions, a godchild is someone who has undergone initiations with a brujo, who is known as the god-father or godmother and becomes the person's spiritual priest, teacher, guide, and mentor.

But this is just one of many instances, and not even the worst that I have seen. Neither side, Haitian nor Dominican, is completely clean in this scenario; the fault lies on both. However, that doesn't negate what does go on. Also, although I have not mentioned this so far, Dominicans also get discriminated against and may be poorly treated in Haiti. However, this tends to happen to a lesser degree, as most Dominicans don't generally travel to Haiti, because of its higher poverty, unless with very specific purpose. Therefore, generally speaking Haitians tend to want to migrate to the Dominican Republic, which is better off economically and ecologically speaking, and not the other way around.

Like many other countries and peoples that have experienced the horrors of slavery, there can be a self-hatred, or rather a downplaying of the African or Haitian part. And like many others whose ancestors suffered thus, the children continue the suffering. This has been described by others as an Anti-Africanism or Anti-Haitianism that exists in the Dominican Republic and within the culture. This is very true and cannot be ignored, but rather brought to light.

It is truly unfortunate. However, with the internet, more and more of this is changing. As more information becomes available and can be dispersed, so can there be acceptance and healing. People are coming to understand themselves and their roots better, bringing growth and stability. As the knowledge of history and how things really came together comes forward and more and more people know their roots, things can begin to shift and change. It is a process, but it is a beautiful one to be a part of.

The 21 Divisions or Dominican Voodoo—What's in a Name?

Because of its colonial past, the Dominican Republic is a stronghold of the Catholic faith, and a large number of Dominicans who practice the 21 Divisions or partake of its ceremonies/rituals still identify as exclusively Catholic. Those involved at deeper levels—Papa Boko, Papa Lwa, and Mama Mambo practitioners—will often be more public about their affiliation but state it aligns with Catholicism rather than working against it. Almost all practitioners identify with the Catholic worldview.

Also looking back to the past under the Spanish and later home rule, practicing Voodoo or serving the Misterios was considered a crime, punishable by a fine, imprisonment, or even death. So it was a dangerous thing and thus the word *Voodoo* was not spoken openly. Lots of reports exist of people being punished when caught practicing Voodoo or serving Misterios and Lwa. There are even more undocumented cases.

But beyond that the vast majority of Dominicans and Caballos de Misterio reject the label of Vodou, Voodoo, or Vudu for other reasons. In the Dominican Republic, such terms are often still associated with evil magic and negative sorcery. They are also associated with Haiti and African influence. Thus the tradition is almost always referred to as the 21 Divisions or Los Misterios. Although this belief is changing slowly with the interconnectedness of the world and greater ease of travel, etc., we practitioners know that it will not take a long time before the change is universal. Dominican Voodoo is more accepted and welcomed within the diaspora where the dominant historical factors are not as ingrained.

But these are not the only two naming options. In some locales, the 21 Divisions is simply called Misterios. Dominican Santeria, Dominican Espiritismo, and Dominican folk religion are other terms. Dominican popular religion and Dominican Catholicism or Folk Catholicism are yet more names. Going by so many names is in part why it has been so hard for outsiders to pin down and understand the 21 Divisions.

The tradition is magico-religious rather than religio-magical. Religio-magical is where the religion comes first and the magic is secondary. The magic happens when the right religious conditions have been set. Once the correct religious rituals have been done, magic happens. This is different than magico-religious, where magic is primary and religious practices come secondary, supporting the magical act. They are important in that they are required for successful magic and its achievements.

Lastly, there is no standardized spelling for the word most frequently spelled "Voodoo." Other spellings also exist, which may be intended as synonyms but may also indicate different traditions. There isn't one consistent "correct" spelling. Voodoo remains the most widely recognized and commonly used spelling, and you'll see it in this book's subtitle. However, it is not without controversy. While "Voodoo" may be used very respectfully to identify specific traditions associated with New Orleans, it is also the spelling used in exploitative, cinematic depictions of African religion, as well as in racist diatribes. That spelling has developed a life of its own, frequently used in contexts that have nothing to do with African-based religious traditions, such as "voodoo economics." Because it is so frequently used disrespectfully, that spelling has developed very negative connotations, especially for many practitioners. For these reasons, Vodou, as used in the text of this book, has evolved into the preferred and respectful spelling.

The Brujo

The *brujo* is the priest, the connecting point between the people and the Misterios. He is a necessary intermediary for people to get the help they need from the Misterios. Only the brujo has direct contact, communication, and communion with the Misterios because he has developed the connection and ability to work with the power to create magic and change. A general practitioner can be a servant and child of the Misterios, but may or may not be able to communicate on their own in a clear path or receive the spirits' communication. This is the case for most people. Likewise their power to affect others and achieve change will be limited to varying degrees.

The brujo is also the conduit for the power. His Misterios have the capacity to affect other people in specific ways. He serves with his body and life the Misterios so that others can have the chance to interact with them and receive their aid. He understands the language of the Misterios and their communications. The brujo relies upon his relationship to the Misterios as the source of power to help his clients. Thus, brujos vary in how powerful they are. The more powerful ones are often known as *grande* or *big*. They have a large followings and many people they serve. Also although I will talk about brujos as him, there are female brujas as well.

The Misterios take an active role in all the undertakings of the brujo, and this is central to the brujo's success. The brujo must first consult with the Misterios to find the path and solution. Unlike in many other traditions where the acceptance or agreement of the spirits is assumed as long as the rites are properly conducted, in the 21 Divisions there must be an open dialogue between the brujo and the Misterios where the answers are received.

As with everything in this tradition, there are a number of terms that may be employed for a priest of the 21 Divisions. The term we will use, *brujo*, literally means "witch." Clearly it is a loaded word, particularly from a Catholic viewpoint. Some may use it in a derogatory manner, implying a person is practicing evil or black magic. But it can also be used to imply great power. It is not uncommon to also see the same person throwing it out as a slur then turning around and referring to himself as a brujo. Keep in mind *brujo* is used in many other Spanish-speaking countries to refer to a witch or a shaman, so it is important to understand that someone can call themselves a brujo but not be a priest of the 21 Divisions.

Another word that's often used is *curioso*, meaning "curious one" or a person who has curiosity about the other world, the spiritual realm. A *faculto* is another term I used to hear in my early years of serving the Misterios, which means "to have the faculties or abilities for" and is implied to mean "to see and work with the spiritual realm." *Curandero* means "healer" or "folk healer." An *espiritista* is a spiritual medium. I've also seen the term *santero* as one who "works with the saints." All of these terms can show up when the environment is less friendly toward spiritual traditions; they have fewer negative associations and connotations.

Lastly, *Papa Boko* and *Mama Mambo* are a male and female priest, respectively, initiated within a lineage. A lineage is a group of people who can trace their origins to a common group of master brujos whose ancient secret rituals, knowledge, and teachings have been passed down from generation to generation. Both the terms *Boko* and *Mambo* come from the African and Haitian elements of Dominican Voodoo. *Boko* carries the meaning of a black magic sorcerer in many areas in Haiti, although in some it simply means a magician or sorcerer. *Boko* comes from the West African Vodou word *Bokono* for the diviner-healer-priest-witch of the West African Vodoun. Only he is able to receive, interpret, and impart the secret messages of the Vodou, the West African Vodoun gods. He was literally the mouthpiece of the secret messages of the gods.

Papa Lwa and *Mama Lwa* are also very old terms, rarely used anymore, but refer to the fact that the brujo brings the Lwa forth like a father or mother and is responsible for caring for them as such. These terms are usually only known to actual initiates themselves or those on that road.

You'll also see that it's common for practitioners to refer to themselves as Catholic. Many see themselves as being religiously Catholic and spiritual practitioners of the Misterios. This doesn't cause conflict for the practitioners themselves. Rather, they see that it goes hand in hand and works together. Thus practitioners are frequently found attending church as well as Voodoo rituals. This is something peculiar and specific to Dominican Voodoo. As previously discussed, many brujos are genuine believers in the Catholic faith and have undergone or undergo the various Catholic sacraments of baptism, holy communion, confession, and so on. In fact, a common joke is that the majority of brujos are better and more diligent Catholics than the general population of the faithful. Many brujos share a Catholic moral code and believe in the miracles of the Church and the saints, the reception of the sacraments, etc.

Some may deny serving the Misterios. This is because it's well known and documented that making such claims in certain areas can lead to prison, physical harm to the brujo or his family, and even death. The culture in the Dominican Republic has always been ambivalent toward the practice. In many areas it's seen as a savage practice that is tolerated and a blind eye is turned "as long as it doesn't get too out of hand."

This is slowly changing thankfully. Nevertheless, due to knowledge and education, more and more brujos are claiming their positions and standing strong. Many brujos are a source of charity and help for their communities. Brujos have always been the doctors, psychologists, priests, healers, shamans of the people. The brujo often wears many hats and fulfills many roles. The brujo is able to come in and help where many others have failed or where nothing but God and the Misterios will be able to make a change.

The Aplasa: A Brujo's Right Hand

The *aplasa*—when a brujo works with one—is the main assistant to the brujo and his Misterios. One of my teachers used to say, "The aplasa knows more than the brujo, because he is always the one sitting with the Misterios." This individual knows the brujo's Misterios intimately and how they like to be attended when they arrive.

The aplasa's job is to placate and serve the Misterio. He makes sure that everything that the Misterio needs is ready. The aplasa also serves as an interpreter for the clients and people who come to receive from the Misterios. Aside from the language of people, the Misterios have their own way of communicating and also use particular gestures. In fact, how a Misterio interacts and behaves during a possession is just as important a part of the message as what is said.

Not all brujos work with an aplasa or with one all the time. Some only employ aplasas during larger events or ceremonies, working alone the rest of the time. An aplasa is not usually paid; the blessings received from attending the Misterios are thanks enough. However, if much work is going on, the brujo does usually give his aplasas some contribution. An aplasa is usually only employed if the Misterios will be called to mount the brujo. Aplasas may or may not be initiates but are chosen by the Misterios to assist the brujo.

The Brujo's Workshop

The *bayi*, or altar room, is where the brujo conducts his rituals. It may also be spelled *badji* or *baji*. Another common name is *santuario* or sanctuary. Depending on the status of the brujo, this may be a whole room or just a corner of a room. The focal point of the bayi is the altar, which is both a portal to the spiritual world and a meeting place. It is an intersection where the spiritual and the physical worlds come together and interact.

The altar usually consists of either a four-legged table or shelves at various heights. The table may also have various shelves built upon it, to give it varying levels. The table is most often covered with an altar cloth. Images of the various saints that are associated with the different Lwases will be placed along the back wall of the altar, creating a space for each Misterio on the table. On the floor under or near the altar will go the altars to certain divisions that prefer to be served on the ground. The altar will have rosaries, candles, flowers, and various bottles of drinks for libations and offerings to the spirits. The altar will usually have a mix of fresh and artificial flowers. There may be food offerings or magical workings on the table. The *plato divisional*, or divisional plate, which holds the sacred foods of all the spirits, is also consistently present on the altar.

Many altars focus on a large central cross. Some have the three crosses, which are known as *calvario*, or the calvary. The three crosses have special significance and undergo rituals that make the portals to various spiritual realms. The altar also will have a glass of water and a bell. All in all, the altar has a very Catholic appearance. Except for the drinks and occasional items that pass through the altar, as they are being used, it would be very difficult for anyone to know that this is a Voodoo altar. A table with saints, rosaries, candles, and flowers is a normal sight in any Catholic church. Along with all of that, you will also find in the room clothing for the spirits if the brujo uses them. Other spiritual tools or materials for magical workings may be about.

Tools of the Brujo

The most important tool of the brujo is the *panuelo*, or kerchief, also known as *fula*. Each Misterio that the brujo works with will have these sacred cloths in their colors. The Misterios usually tie these on their head or somewhere on the body once they have mounted the brujo. Each Misterio can be identified simply by the fulas they wear and how. The brujo is also able to make many miracles happen for people by use of the panuelos. Panuelos can be employed for protection, to cleanse with certain forces, and in healings.

Another big tool of the brujo is cigars. Cigars are used in divinations, cleansings, and even to remove negative spirits. Most commonly, they are smoked to call or invoke the Misterios to mount or do some other spiritual work. Sacred to the Caribbean natives, tobacco is used to bring about the state needed to be mounted by Lwases. It's not uncommon to see brujos smoking cigars incessantly or with other brujos.

The bell on the altar is always used to work with the spirits. If the brujo belongs to a Tcha Tcha lineage, he will shake this sacred rattle in conjunction with his bell. This rattle is a gourd on a stick. It is used particularly by those in that lineage mainly or to call upon Indian spirits. However, not all brujos use the rattle. Most brujos also have a rosary or a number of rosaries that they utilize in the sacred work.

Finally, there is the *Jarro Divisional,* which is a sacred vessel. After a certain level of development and rituals have been completed, the brujo receives this object from the Misterios of the brujo's teacher. This vessel contains a secret sacred liquid with immense power. It is made of a metal or an enamelware cup that looks like a coffee mug with handle. It has seven ribbons of various colors tied around its base, and when it is in use, the brujo sticks a lit candle on the handle.

That makes up the main tools of the brujo. In truth a brujo needs very little in order for his Misterios to work miracles. Aside from these main tools and the altar, the brujo will use a variety of herbs, powders, oils, perfumes, liquids, potions, candles, oil lamps, and more when making magic or doing treatments.

In Dominican Voodoo, servidores, who are not brujos, aren't allowed to keep such altars. Instead they are allowed to keep a household altar, which has a very specific way of being built, which we'll get to later. Likewise, only certain types of offerings are allowed to servidores. This is because the Misterios, although good, are also powerful and dangerous. So it's better to not keep an altar than to have one and not properly care for it. Also, in order to actually have the capacity to properly care for an altar, one has to have undergone a certain level of spiritual preparation. One's godparent or Papa should also be a consistent guiding light on its care for the budding brujo to develop properly.

How the Brujo Becomes a Brujo

In the 21 Divisions, a person can be or be called to become a brujo in a number of ways. The most common is that a brujo is called to be one at birth. The truth is all brujos are born to be brujos, they all just undergo the process differently. So when we say at birth, we mean that the brujo is immediately recognized by others, or he recognizes himself, as being one or realizes his different nature from an early age. In the Dominican Republic, there are a number of signs that tell the mother she may be pregnant with a child who has otherworldly powers. Likewise there are indications of a child being a brujo that very often show up during childhood. Young and even child Caballos de Misterios and brujos are not uncommon in the 21 Divisions.

The brujo is not a normal everyday individual: he is a magical being incarnated, which at times brings immense awe, love, and fear in those around him. One of the signs and characteristics marking a brujo is a strong capacity to enter trances—usually involuntarily, at least in the beginning. Another mark is a certain look in the eyes, and again they may or may not be aware of it. The personality of the brujo is markedly different from those in his peer group even early on. Paranormal and otherworldly happenings commonly occur around brujos, especially in youth. Born with a connection to the Misterios and a strong connection to God and the Mysteries of God, brujos have different innate capacities that are not the same as others.

The powers can also be inherited from or given to the person by a spirit or a relative. A Misterio can give the power and call a person to be a brujo at any point.

Lastly, the magical arts and certain spiritual power can be developed and acquired through study, although, as you'll see, once they've received the call all brujos are required to undergo study and development of their power. The calling alone is not enough but just the mark that the brujo is ready to start the path. Becoming the brujo or awakening to one's nature or mission is really only the beginning of the journey.

Many of the ways in which the brujo is called into service are often intertwined and mixed. The calling can come by many routes. Common ways include a deep illness, being mounted by the spirits, sudden suffering that doesn't have any trace, or intense anxiety, nervousness, and an uncomfortable disposition that can't be controlled. Issues with blacking out, rage, and character control and development are another means. Intense illnesses that can only be cured spiritually or are cured by a spiritual visitation or callings via a dream or vision are common. Suddenly being possessed by a spirit, Misterios or otherwise, is a clear indication of an innate ability. Tragedy may also strike the brujo's life in order to awaken him to his true purpose. These aren't the only ways. No matter the means, all are usually accompanied by strange dreams, phenomena, and revelations. The brujo-to-be may also be called via dreams and visions where the spirits interact with him, tell him of his calling, or do any number of things. The calling comes by the grace of God. There is nothing else that can bring it forward. Once it is heard, it cannot be shut out.

Once they are called, these individuals will start to look for a master brujo for guidance. This will start, as all things do, with a consulta. Once the brujo is found to guide the one called, this person will be known as the Padrino/Papa, if male, or Madrina/Mama, if female. The main Misterios of the individual usually want some degree of unravelment before traveling further along the path. The new brujo will be given various tasks and spiritual obligations to complete—each one unraveling la fuerza more. The brujo will be taught many things by his Misterios. This is one of the marks of the brujo: the Misterios themselves teach the brujo "how to work."

Process of Initiation

Once the brujo has been able to accomplish the initial unravelment set by his head Misterio, a time will come when the Misterios will give the go-ahead for the start of the formal initiation process.

Initiation is not taken lightly in the culture. Aside from the powers the brujo-to-be will have, he will also have responsibilities. Initiation creates a formal relationship of honor, respect, and power, but also duty. He will no longer live the normal life—his will be dedicated to God, the Misterios, and a higher purpose. Once initiated, there is no going back. Not fulfilling your sacred responsibilities can lead to illness, harm, or even death to you and your loved ones. The Misterios are dangerous and finicky. It's very common for the brujo to resist the call and the process.

Deep down his spirit knows what it means. No matter how much he resists, though, the only way he will live well is to serve his Divine purpose.

In Dominican Voodoo, the aim of initiation is not status or title. Initiation doesn't make a priest. Rather it's through initiation that the priest discovers, develops, connects to, and is given control over his power. The goal therefore of initiation in Dominican Voodoo is to develop the person's spiritual power—this and creating strong connections and passages to the Misterios the initiation will provide.

Not all servidores or brujos are initiated. But all brujos undergo training and learning from their Misterios in order to develop power. They will also serve as a portal to the Misterios. The main thing is the spiritual force the brujo has with his Misterios and his capacity to work for people. Those brujos who are not initiated, however, are not able to initiate others, do not have access to certain secrets, and do not perform certain types of rituals. Since they have not received initiation, it is not something they can pass on. Likewise, they are limited in their capacity to teach and take on apprentices. Uninitiated brujos should focus only on healing and magic for clients.

Through initiation, the Padrino connects the Misterios directly to the brujo-to-be. The Padrino works on improving the brujo as a portal and vessel to the Misterios. The bond between the brujo-to-be and his Misterios is sealed, and that starts to unravel his power at an unparalleled pace. The stronger the relationship and bond between the brujo and his Misterios, the more powerful he becomes. The Misterios teach their brujos many secrets and empower them more and more.

However, initiation alone will not be the only challenge the new brujo will face. The Misterios themselves will also charge him with tasks to complete and lessons to learn. The brujo must be mindful to follow all the requirements of the Misterios, lest his relationship with them weakens. The tests of the Misterios won't just be spiritual.

The brujo undergoes an arduous initiation process to unravel his powers. He is also always in the process of growing them more and more. The journey of initiation into the 21 Divisions works like a ladder, meaning one goes up one step at a time. There may be instances when one is able to hop up two steps in one go; however, for the most part it is a process that takes its time and years. True power requires room to develop and then eventually control; only then can you be at the foot of the Mountain of Mastery.

Learning from his Misterios and his Padrino, the brujo will develop and master how to properly use his new powers. Three types of power or force exist, and through initiation and development the brujo will learn to control them all. Various levels of initiation build the relationship and align the brujo with his Misterios more and more. In Dominican Voodoo, there are three major initiations a servidor can undergo and each one is designed to take the person deeper into the power. There are also numerous other initiations and rituals with more specific aims and goals.

The first initiation is known as *refresco de cabeza* or refreshing the head. This ceremony clears the connection between the individual and his Misterio de Cabeza—the main Misterio who owns the brujo's head and will be the main Misterio he will work with. During the ceremony, the initiate's head will be washed with various *refrescos*, or sodas, along with other materials. Strengthening the powers of the Misterio de Cabeza, the refrescos increase the servidor's capacity to receive from the Lwa. The ceremony also assists in the development of trance possession, making it more frequent. It opens and enhances psychic and spiritual abilities, unraveling and strengthening the connection. This ceremony usually spans a few hours. During this time, the Papa or Mama will call and mount the spirits. The Lwa will perform secret rites on the person to open their head and consciousness to the Head Misterio. Fulas will be consecrated at the same time for the new initiate to work with continuing on the path.

The *aplasamiento* placates the Misterios of the initiate. It's the second stage of the process of connection with power. It builds up the foundation so that the brujo's power stabilizes and grows strong. Now, other Lwases that are with the brujo will be connected, established, and fed. This gives the brujo access to a larger base of power. Aside from that, the brujo will be given various magical protections to aid him and stop any magical attacks sent his way. This ceremony is also done when a Caballo de Misterio, horse of the spirits, has violent or overly frequent possessions. You'll notice that the name *aplasamiento* has the root word *aplasa*, which is also the title of a brujo's assistant. *Apalsar* means "to placate" and "to help relax or ease into its position." An aplasa, however, doesn't necessarily have to have undergone this ritual. Assistants to the brujo may or may not be initiated, although they are usually apprenticing to some degree or have a strong connection to the brujo. Both the aplasa and the aplasamiento work to placate and provide the foundations needed for the Misterios. This ritual can span between one and three days.

The *bautizo* is the last major initiation that the brujo will undergo. This ceremony connects him to all of the 21 Divisions, consecrating him into all the major rites. Only a brujo who has taken this stage of initiation will eventually have the ability to call him- or herself a Papa Boko or Mama Mambo. The ceremony doesn't confer the title, rather it gives permission for the title to be bestowed when the time is right. In Dominican Voodoo, this title is given to brujos who will serve others with their power. It can only be given by the Misterios of the Papa or Mama of the brujo. When this title is given, it means the person has earned and developed the capacity to work for others. The bautizo seals the pact between the brujo and his Misterios. His powers unfold and blossom at an accelerated pace. In time, the brujo will tap into his full power with dedication and steadiness on the path. He will receive many empowerments and protections.

Aside from the brujo's Padrino or Papa, there will be anywhere from one to three other assistants, also brujos, who will oversee or support the rituals. This process can take from three to nine days, depending on the lineage of the master. Some brujos only conduct this ceremony in the Dominican Republic for various reasons. Although this ceremony can be and is done all over the world, provided that the materials can be attained, it's seen as better carried out in the homelands of the tradition, also known as *Tierra Caliente* or the Hot Land, because of the Misterios' origins there. In some cases, like the Indians, some of the Misterios actually walked that very same land. Therefore, the land is "hot" because it's filled with magical powers.

During the rituals, the initiate will be taken to various natural locations, home of the Misterios, and receive ceremonies there. The brujo will go to the woods for the Petroses, the cemetery for the Black Division, and the river for the Division of the Sweet Waters. This ceremony will have many servicios to all of the various major groups. Some lineages will sacrifice animals at this time, binding the pact with blood. The brujo's Misterios will also be called to mount him and reveal their secrets. The bautizo concludes with a small ceremony of close family and friends, in which the new brujo's Misterios will be honored and called into possession. The Misterios of other brujos in attendance will also come to congratulate the new initiate. Once finished, the brujo will go home with all of the sacred tools received during the ceremony.

He will also receive various puntos—or spiritual focuses—of Misterios to further his progress and development as he grows spiritually. Each will unravel his various spiritual powers and capacities, aligning him with his Misterios and creating a strong bond that will be part of the brujo's strength forever. There will be tests to his ego—psychological, mental, and emotional tests, and tests of commitment and dedication to his Misterios. The Misterios will have demands not only on what the brujo does spiritually, but also whom he associates and deals with, his relationships, what he does and doesn't say, and so on. If the brujo follows their guidance diligently, his power will continuously grow. If he does not, his power will stagnate and wither.

As my aunt would say: "Each brujo pays for his power one way or the other, for the good or for the bad."

At times, individuals from outside of the culture who have sought to enter the tradition have run after getting the bautizo as fast as possible with the belief that status can be attained or the desire for great power sated immediately. You'll never see this from people within the culture, and for good reason—it's harmful and detrimental. Receiving ceremonies that bring on this level of power without proper training and development can and often does lead to illness, chaos, accidents, psychosis and psychological issues, and even death. It's too much for the system of the person, and the damage can be the equivalent to frying out an electrical box.

Puntos: Points of Power

A *punto* literally means "a point." But what it actually speaks of in our tradition is any concentrated point of spiritual power. As such, it is one of the most commonly used terms in the 21 Divisions. A punto can have or not have a physical counterpart. In other words, there may or may not be a physical object. The concentrated point of power usually condenses a spiritual force. Puntos can be placed in different locations, they can be made to concentrate the power of a spirit or Misterio, and they can be tied to things or people. We also use the phrase *giving puntos* during a ceremony, which refers to certain rituals or spiritual actions that are done in order to draw forth more of the same power and connect it. We can also "give puntos" to the Misterios, meaning giving them certain services or rituals in order to create magic or change.

A punto can also be an initiation ceremony, though not all puntos are initiations. It doesn't carry the same weight as the three main initiations we've just discussed. During such a ritual, the brujo will give the punto of a specific Lwa, division, or power. This is known as giving someone the punto of Anaisa or the punto of Metresili, and so on. A punto draws in, ties, and connects the person with that particular spirit or force. A punto is also permanent. The purpose of receiving a punto this way can be varied; however, it's usually for spiritual growth, development, and connection, or as a type of treatment when there is a need for healing or correcting major energetic or life imbalances. During the major initiations the brujo will undergo, such as the aplasamiento and bautizo, many puntos will be shared. In some lineages, the bautizo is not done at all, rather a brujo goes through twenty-one puntos, though this is not common.

Making Magic and Miracles: Spiritual Work

How the Brujo Works

Most rituals in Dominican Voodoo are private, solely consisting of the brujo, his client, and an assistant or two—aplasas—if the brujo works with any. Public rituals are not the norm and are usually only held once a year or every so many years for the brujo to serve and properly care for his Misterios. These are usually put on near the feast days of the saints corresponding to each Lwa. For example, a brujo whose main Misterio is Belie Belcan would host a San Miguel Ceremony on the feast of St. Michael, September 29. The brujo may also host smaller private rituals and ceremonies for his clients collectively.

Brujos most often work in one of two ways. The first is *avista clara*, meaning "clear-eyed." The brujo relies upon his spiritual powers only to communicate with the Misterios and then relays the information and messages to his client(s). Falling into a trance, he sees the spirits, hears their messages, and is told what is going on. A Misterio may also choose to speak through him or channel through the brujo's voice. In this form, the Misterios will ring a bell when controlling their horse. The Misterios interject whenever necessary, changing the voice, tonality, and pitch while revealing information.

The second way is known as *montado* or *montao*, meaning "mounted." In this method, the spirits are called into possession. They will agree to assist and leave instructions to be completed by the horse or petitioner. A person who works montao will also work avista clara, but not necessarily the other way around. The foundation of all is a brujo's development of *fuerza,* or spiritual power—no matter what method is being used—which allows him to channel and work with the Misterios and the forces they bring in.

The brujo's capacity to be a direct channel for the power as well as his ability to then use it makes the brujo a sorcerer extraordinaire. Dominican Voodoo and its brujos are known far and wide for the most intense and powerful magical workings. In fact, in 2004 I traveled to Poland, having been hired to do some magical works there. The people who hired me had me come and stay for three weeks. Apparently, they had been doing so with a Dominican bruja for many years, but as she was by then elderly and no longer willing to travel, she referred them to me. She would usually come there with a few cloths, a rosary, and a bell. She would ask them to provide certain items for her Misterios to partake of, drinks and smokes, and she was ready to work for them spiritually. Seeing that I had brought the same exact things, they told me this. Upon returning home to the United States, I paid her a visit with a huge grocery, some gifts for her main Misterio San Miguel, and some things from the people back in

Poland. It was beautiful to see our tradition blossoming around the globe thanks to many hardworking brujos.

Consulta: Consultation with the Spirits

Either way the brujo works, the *consulta*, or consultation, is the very first step. In this meeting the brujo investigates the client's issues or problems at hand, uncovering the trouble and finding the proper solution. The brujo can conduct the consultation avista clara using various forms of divination, such as reading cards, tea leaves, or cigars as well.

He may also do the consultation with the Misterios in possession or montado. This is known as *llamando Misterios*—calling the Misterio—or *consulta con Misterio*—consultation with the Misterio. Sessions with the Misterios usually start in the following manner: After various purifications and preparations, usually days in advance, the brujo begins by doing final cleansings to prepare his body to receive the spirit. Then the brujo begins making invocations, prayers, and calling the Lwa. This may be accompanied by music, bells, or the shaking of the sacred rattle known as the tcha tcha. Eventually his body begins to tremble as the process takes place. Once the Lwa has arrived, he will be given his *panuelo* and drinks and smokes, along with whatever his or her other accoutrements may be. Alternately, the brujo may have outfitted himself with these prior to calling the Misterio. In this fashion, the Misterio is already outfitted upon his arrival. Once settled, the Lwa begins to consult.

During the consultation, the spirit will explain and expound upon the client's problems and issues. The Lwa may advise and prophesy for the client. Usually the Lwa will prescribe the solution and remedy for the person's issues through rituals, spells, spiritual work, magical workings, ceremonies, initiations, healings, a spiritual bath or treatment, a specific action or set of tasks, or any combination of the above and much more. Sometimes, yet less commonly, the Lwa will do the work for the client or some other treatments. Once the solution has been given, the Lwa will then leave and the brujo will return to normal. At this point the brujo may start the work on the solution or may have the client set another appointment for that. Most brujos keep a bit of the supplies for their most common workings. But if other specific items are needed that aren't on hand, the client will need to procure them and bring this to the brujo to do the work—although some brujos choose to procure these items for their clients instead.

The brujo usually has a certain Misterio that he calls in for consulting with his clients. Some brujos have a broader ability and are able to call in a number of Misterios. It's not uncommon for one or more than one Lwa to come during such times. Consultations with the Lwases are usually held every so often and most often done for a number of clients collectively. However, clients can and do book private sessions with the Misterios. Many brujos only do consultations with Misterios and magical works on certain days of the week. There are many magical and spiritual reasons behind this.

Getting Help from the Brujo

None of the brujo's services are free. The brujo is like any other professional—whether doctors, lawyers, or accountants—and has trained extensively in order to work with the Misterios to help others. He has spent countless hours and time and money refining and developing his gifts. The payment for the consultation is one part of what he receives and only includes the consultation itself. Recommended magical works, servicios, and other treatments are separate and paid for as such.

The cost of services varies greatly from brujo to brujo. It will be based on the skill, expertise, and power of the brujo. Because of these variables, the cost of the same ritual can be very different from one brujo to another. The cost of seeing the top doctor is definitely different than seeing the local doctor. Generally speaking, the consulta is the least expensive service that a brujo will offer.

Servicios: Resolving with the Misterios

Servicios, meaning "services," are one of the most common and foundational practices within the 21 Divisions. Though there are many types of servicios and the word is often used in a general way, many servicios often focus on offerings made in the form of food, candle, drink, and other special items. The relationship between the Misterios and humans is that "one hand washes the other"—each side serving and helping the other. Servicios are a common prescription to a problem once a consultation has been held. Many issues can be diagnosed as an imbalance with one of the Misterios. Therefore, by making the proper services to the Misterios, the issue can be corrected.

Servicios are also used for the regular care of the Misterios. Every servidor de Misterio, brujo or not, has a responsibility to his Misterios, especially once they have undergone the various initiations, and making proper servicios is one of them. Servicios ensure that the servidor's life and power are flowing properly. Servidores check in with a consulta to find out what their Misterios need. Servicios most often feature some type of food offering along with candles and other gifts that the Lwa may take with it. Each Misterio has specific Servicios that are used to work with that Misterio in particular ways.

Servicios can also be given to appease an offended or upset Misterio. A Misterio can become offended when rituals are not carried out properly or by a person with the proper capacity, when a promise is broken, or when you have acted without honor and respect. One can also offend the Misterios by offending others in one's community and living a life that is not congruent with them. The Misterios act as Divine agents. Forgetting a Misterio or one's responsibilities can also cause the Misterio to become angry with you. Some individuals require regular servicios to certain Misterios to correct certain imbalances they have.

Servicios are given to maintain protection, safety from danger, blessings, and luck from the Misterios. They can also be given to make a particular petition to achieve some specific goal or blessing. In this way, the servicio works to find favor with the Misterio so that the desire can be achieved. Likewise, many servicios offer thanks for a goal or blessing that has been given as payment to a promise or because the person has achieved a magical goal. Sometimes they are a part of a magical contract that was created by the person, the brujo, and the Misterios.

Misterios respond to servicios by changing the energy to attract the desired goal. Through the proper service, the Misterio brings forth and multiplies the power to make miracles happen. However, they will not have the same results even when conducted exactly the same by two different people. Nevertheless, many servicios are magical in nature, following a particular type of recipe in order to attain specific results or special favors. For some, all work done with the Misterio falls under the title "servicio." In the servicios are many secrets of power. Knowing the servicios, how to do them, and when to do them makes up a major part of a brujo's training. Servicios can bring balance, health, strength, and protection. Certain servicios may be placed by the brujo in the client's house or need regular maintenance and care by the person or brujo. Then there are servicios that keep food in the home, protect and guard, chase away evil, and many others that may be placed in a certain environment. Servicios are among the many things that may be referred to as puntos, as in "I put some puntos for Metresili," meaning I gave some special and specific offerings to Metresili.

Magic and Brujeria: Dominican Spells and Magic

We can't speak of the 21 Divisions or Dominican Voodoo without discussing magic. Magic is the capacity to change events according to what one desires. It is a gift, a skill, and an art. A brujo works to become master of the triad that it takes to create successful change.

In truth, all of life is magic, and magic is a part of the very essence of life. Servidores de Misterio are always on the lookout for signs coming from the Misterios. Nothing goes unnoticed, and the universe and the Mysteries are regularly and constantly trying to communicate where they stand with us. By looking and being aware, the brujo sees what forces are at play and how to best navigate in order to achieve desired ends.

In the 21 Divisions, doing well spiritually will manifest in blessings, luck, and success physically. Issues and problems in the physical world often indicate deeper issues in the spiritual realm. Thus, if someone has power, it shows through how they live, act, and are. If a person lacks power, it will likewise manifest through them. Having power is about having the force to resolve, overcome, and be strong in doing so. It also includes minimizing and preventing risks, dangers, and harm, but this doesn't mean negative things will never happen. So you can see that having power doesn't necessarily equate to experiencing no problems or issues; rather a person of power has the capacity to resolve issues in a manner that is beneficial and favorable. In actuality, a person with power will often find themselves dealing with *more* than someone without. Being called to use and wield power can bring about its own issues. It is this unused power in need of an outlet that calls to the brujo.

Many people get confused when it comes to magic. The recipe does not determine the magic's success. It is the capacity of the practitioner to channel and wield the power that determines the outcome of the spell. A more powerful practitioner can complete complex spells with little to no supporting items. This all depends on the person's relationship and connection, and where they stand with their Misterios. This is important to understand. Do not to confuse the capacity of the brujo with the capacity of the Misterios. For example, two brujos can both work with Belie Belcan. And one can resolve for you what the other can't. It's not due to Belie Belcan's range of power but rather the capacity of the brujo through which Belie Belcan is working. This is why the most serious brujos are always expanding and learning from their elders and the Misterios. The Caballo de Misterio is regularly being trained by the Misterios to be able to carry more and bring through more spiritual force and power.

This is well understood in the 21 Divisions and Dominican culture. For that reason, although there are many traditional spells one could get one's hands on and attempt, most Dominicans prefer to go to a brujo. As my aunt would say: "A layman trying spiritual work is like a child playing doctor." There are countless secrets that brujos have when it comes to working magic and many that only brujos have access to. Aside from this, the brujo's training and development have built the capacity to send enormous amounts of power into a situation. A brujo's popularity and fame are based on his ability to achieve success with magic and healing. The more powerful the brujo, the stronger his Misterios will come through. The more powerful the Misterios are, the stronger the brujo can train to be within his capacity or abilities.

The next thing to understand about magic is that it follows natural and universal laws. Magic defies the odds, that is true, but it doesn't break natural and universal laws. The Misterios are also limited by the power and authority given to them by God to do any task. This is known as being given the grace—power and permission—to do whatever act. So, the Misterios do have power, but it is through Divine grace that it can be used. Therefore, just because someone has a desire doesn't automatically mean it can be accomplished. This is why the consultation is such a necessary first step.

Within our magic, there are two types of recipes. In my lineage, we call these two types of recipes *traditional* and *spiritual*. Traditional recipes are known by the general public. They can sometimes be found in botanicas and in prayer books. These are often considered safe for a layperson to perform. Spiritual recipes, on the other hand, are given directly to brujos by the Misterios. These recipes vary from one brujo to another, one case to another, depending on the factors at play. Lastly, brujos that are initiated into a lineage also have secret recipes from that lineage. These recipes have been handed down like family recipes.

Limpiezas, or spiritual cleansings, are very important to both the brujo and his clients. Limpiezas remove negative energy and spiritual grime. They are the hygiene of the spirit; just as the body requires regular care and cleansing, so does one's spiritual body. Negative energy is often the source of sudden issues and problems, therefore servidores de Misterios and other spiritual people always make sure to keep themselves spiritually clean. Over time, negative energy left unresolved can cause greater blockages, illnesses, and accidents.

Firstly, magical works are known as *trabajos*, or *trabajos espirituales*, which basically means "spiritual work." Another word for a magical spell is *wanga*. In some places wanga specifically means black magic, however. Servicios can be the central point of magic, accompany it, or can be made after as payment to the Misterios. These offerings alter and manipulate the forces of life and how they manifest. Among some brujos, all magical works are referred to as servicios especially when they end up on the altar. Many works you'll find are titled by what they do or how they are done.

Magical baths are central to many brujos' work. Whenever possible, people prefer to have the bath administered by the brujo, or at least the first bath if there are to be many over a course of days. Again, they ask this because of the spiritual power and forces that the brujo has greater access to, and thus the bath is stronger. If a person is to take many baths, such as over the course of days, they will take the preparation home with them to self-administer the remaining days. Magical baths are prepared using herbs, perfumes, oils, and other ingredients. The magic is absorbed through the aura and skin of the person receiving the spiritual bath.

Some magical works are designed to "heat" things up. This is to bring movement—more action, activity, passion, anger, and progress in a situation. Then there are works to cool things down— slow down situations, calm anger, and tranquilize issues between people. *Revocacciones*, or revocations, are made to return or turn back magic to sender as well as to cancel negative magical effects.

Resguardos are magical protections. They can be made to protect against any number of conditions. Some are worn on the person like a talisman or amulet. Others are drunk in a potion or brew. Yet others are administered in ceremonies. One can be protected against one's enemies, the police, gunshots, magical attacks, envy, and much more depending on what has been received.

In court cases, the side with the brujo and his Misterios is the one that wins. Everyone knows that. Brujos are able to manifest all sorts of incredible occurrences through the power of the Misterios. Opposing legal teams, witnesses, and others are dumbfounded, grow confused, or make major mistakes. Sweetening the judge and jury to the client, people changing their minds, paperwork going missing, cases being totally dismissed or closed out for no reason, jail sentences cut by half or even more, and all sorts of miraculous turnarounds can happen.

Naturally brujos are experts at business, job, and money magic. Many techniques exist for making businesses thrive, crushing the competition, and bringing forth success.

Dealing with spirits and spiritual issues, such as negative entities or beings, is not undertaken by many brujos. When it comes to dealing with the dead and other malevolent spirits, there is danger for the brujo and a whole lot of work, although the client may actually only be witnessing 10 percent of what the brujo has to do. Initiation and being a spiritual guru, teacher, or parent is another realm that is not for all. For the Misterios this is a major responsibility on the part of all parties. Being a spiritual guide requires a great deal of patience, understanding, compassion, and love. There must be a willingness to sacrifice and put others before self. No brujo undertakes this lightly, knowing that in the spiritual world, among the Misterios, agreements are also being made by the Misterios of teacher and student. The bond of the spirit is greater than the ties of blood or water. For your spirit will never evaporate. For this reason, it's so important to choose and move wisely whenever it comes to this.

In the realms of love magic, there are various types of spells with various aims. *Endulcimientos*, or sweetenings, are made to smooth things out between a couple, heightening sweetness, love, and good feelings for the petitioner. *Amarres*, or binding spells, are very popular. The word *amarres* is often misused and misunderstood. Often a person will call the work an amarres or try to do an amarres to return a lover. This is ineffective. An amarres is used to tie a person and a good situation. You cannot tie something that you don't have. Also, if you tie a situation while it's negative, you tie the negativity into it. This creates a cyclical problem.

Brujos are also extremely well versed in the creation of powerful potions and brews. In fact, many spells are done through the working of potions. There are potions that are drunk, others that are applied on the self or target, and yet others that are disposed of in various ways or have servicios that are used to make them work. Powders are another popular choice of some brujos, in which the powder is applied in different ways in order to cause the desired effect.

Herbs and plants are often central pieces in the work of many brujos. Because of this, most are herbalists to one extent or the other, although some choose to specialize in herbalism both medicinally and magically. Some brujos also specialize in healing, sometimes referring to themselves as a *curandero/a* or healer. I've met brujos who know how to set bones, dentist brujos, digestive specialist brujos, brujos who specialize in treating mental conditions, and many others. Most have cases of beautiful and miraculous healings that have been performed or witnessed.

Next, we have *enviaciones* or *enviar un Misterio*. This is one of the most powerful methods of magic. In this, the brujo sends a Misterio who then works on the person's behalf or on the case. If it's something that's ongoing or complex, the client will bring the brujo money so that the brujo can make special servicios that keep the Misterio working for the person. The Misterio will go and do whatever it takes to achieve the desire. In this way, the Misterio changes whatever is being done according to what's going on with the situation.

Another method is to make a *promesa,* or promise ceremony. In this, the brujo creates an agreement between the person and the Misterio. The person agrees to make specific offerings and sacrifices once the Lwa gains the desired result. It's common to combine a promesa with other work, as the promesa serves to boost or help things and get the Misterios to work faster. The promesa sacrifice is in addition to the offerings that are normally made when there are magical results.

Division Negra/Black Division

The Black Division is the group of spirits that rule over the Mysteries of Life and Death. They are comprised of the very Mysteries of Death and all the ancestral elevated dead who have become Misterios. The Black Division holds these secrets and is able to teach and reveal them to their servants.

One of the biggest divisions, the Black Division, grows larger and larger regularly as spirits of the dead are elevated and reborn as guiding forces to the living. This division is known for helping people undo and reverse curses, hexes, and other negativity. But it also can assist a servidor to do the same. Since the division is so large and varied, it can assist people to accomplish almost any aim. As can be expected, the majority of these spirits live in the cemetery.

Baron de Cementerio

Baron is the Mystery of Death. He is the king of the cemetery and king of the dead. Baron de Cementerio is seen on the altar with the image of Saint Elijah of Mount Carmel. As Death, he is the gatekeeper of the passage between the physical and spiritual worlds. His symbol is a cross representing the crossing of the physical plane or material world with the spiritual plane and realms. Although Papa Legba, who is the Misterio of doors and gateways, controls the doors to the spirits, Baron is the only other Misterio who holds the same keys. He is the spirit of Death that comes looking for you when your time has come. As such, he is a judge and known for his power to officiate between life and death. Since he is a judge, he will only allow someone to be magically killed if they are guilty.

Baron is worked with by brujos for all types of goals and ends. Through his large and vast network, he is able to achieve any end that a person may seek—one of the other reasons for his great following and popularity. However, due to his nature, he is most often called to destroy obstacles, black magic, and enemies. He has the power to reverse negativity and overcome any defeat.

One of the most popular Misterios among brujos is Baron of the Cemetery. On a Monday, it is a normal thing to see almost a dozen brujos smoking cigars in the cemetery, making offerings and servicios to him. Every cemetery features an altar to him, at least, though many cemeteries also have an altar for all the Misterios. Baron is known for his command over many spirits and for his connections to many of the Lwases and Metresas. His network is huge and his power extends across distance and time. Baron has a sacred space in every cemetery; it is the grave of the first male buried. Usually a cross is placed here along with his altar. That spirit is elevated into the status of a Baron, or caretaker, of that particular cemetery.

However, there is one particular grave of the "Great Baron of the Cemetery" seen to be the actual Baron of the Cemetery. This grave is at a specific site, and brujos often go to attend this grave. It is the resting place of the first man buried in the New World when Christopher Columbus came over and "discovered" it and is seen as the original and first Baron. There are secrets and mysteries to working with this Baron, and due to his power over time, his reputation and magic have grown great.

Baron is like a wind, like air. He is everywhere and near all things, constantly. He is constantly in motion and active. It's something many people, including spiritualists, want to look at and observe. But brujos that know the secrets know the power that is contained in Death. In death, we find the ultimate clock. Baron is the timekeeper of all timekeepers. As old as time, he knows secrets all the way back to the beginning.

"Death is your best friend," Aunt Nere would often say. By this, she meant that Death is constantly with you. It is constantly watching you. Death is intrinsically tied to life in such a powerful way. "Wherever there is Life, there is death," I tell my godchildren. Death is constantly occurring. Each second is but a mini death—the death of the second before it. For death is but one step away, one breath away. Life is marked by the first and the last breath.

Baron is often one of the first Misterios one will encounter on the spiritual path. In fact, many individuals have been brought into the tradition by Baron. Since Death is connected to all people, it is easy for Baron to bring people into the spiritual work. When people first encounter Baron, they may be meeting one of the many Barons that exist. Baron of the Cemetery, as lead, often has other Barons and spirits of the Black Division doing his work.

In my lineage, we still hold the Ancient Secrets of Baron. Unfortunately, this has been lost in many lineages. But during initiation, we transfer the secrets and the power of life and death to the highest levels of brujos. Through our secret rituals, we are able to have the brujo conquer death and gain power over it. As such, he or she is empowered to be able to handle all that comes their way. The brujo becomes the king, like Baron, over the lands of the dead and the lower spirits. He has them at his command at will. This is why in our lineage, the character and the ethic of the brujo has to be well developed. For the power is immense and dangerous in the wrong hands.

Baron is often called upon to make a debtor repay his debt. He is petitioned as an enforcer. When a lender is facing a person who is unwilling to repay him, it is very common for the person to seek the aid of the brujo. The brujo will most often turn to Baron, as Baron will be called to judge in the matter and serve justice. Death, being everywhere, is able to track the person who is trying to get away.

When Baron mounts a Caballo de Misterio, the body of the horse goes stiff as a board. The body will often become cold as death, as a corpse without any life. Carefully, the horse is laid out on the ground. However, at times, he may be laid across a chair. His panuelo is placed to cover the face and upper body, and the people present will begin the prayers. Our Fathers, Hail Marys, and other Catholic prayers are normally recited as Baron is present.

It is not uncommon for Baron to foam at the mouth. His stomach will often rise and vent up, staying stuck there. While this is happening, people will be allowed to go up to Baron and tell their desires in his ear. Baron will take them with him and the peoples' petitions.

If he is on the ground, it is common for the individuals present to walk over Baron's body carefully. This causes all negativity to drop off of the aura and the person to go through the portal that Baron is providing. This removes all obstacles around the person. If the mounting is at a spiritual ceremony, the roads have been officially opened and cleared for things to move forward. If Baron is coming to assist in a spiritual work, the magic or work may begin.

When Baron de Cementerio is in possession, he is completely like a corpse. He doesn't speak or talk. His possessions don't last very long as they serve to open the bridge. It is very common for the horse to become immediately possessed by another Baron or spirit as soon as Baron leaves.

Although Baron de Cementerio is the leader of the division and the most popular of the Barons, there are a number of other Barons within the 21 Divisions. Each Baron takes on a different aspect or role and adds nuances to the spirit of Death and its work.

As leader of the Black Division, he naturally has strong connections and relationships to all its spirits who are seen to work for him. His wife is known as La Barona. You will get to meet her and learn more about her later. His son, Papa Gede, is seen as his right-hand man and main assistant in the care and maintenance of the world of the dead.

He has a great number of *Centinelas*, or Sentinels and Guardians, whom he relies upon to keep him informed and maintain order.

Baron is known for his incredible protection. He can remove and reverse witchcraft with ease. Many will go to him when they are undergoing spiritual attack, as he is able to quickly resolve the problem.

This was the case with Leda.

Leda is now a servidora de Misterios. But this wasn't always the case. Before becoming a servidora, she had seen brujos before and had consultations. But honestly, she had never really been a participant in the spiritual work or on the spiritual path. What really brought her to becoming a servidora was that she had been enduring all sorts of issues and problems with spiritual attacks. She was being spiritually harassed by her husband's lover. This caused her to turn to a brujo for help. Finally, all the spiritual problems and attacks stopped when she petitioned Baron.

Leda says:

"My husband was cheating on me with a woman. I could take that, I could understand that a man is a man. So I didn't really take it seriously, since it has happened before. It just is how things are. I had broken my head before to get him to stop, but I had been told by a brujo before that he had strong Misterios, so spiritual work on him would be pointless and this was a part of his character that would just never go away. So this woman started to spiritually attack me to get me and my husband to separate. She wanted my husband for herself. I started suffering from insomnia and nervousness. This is not how I am. I've always been a very calm and tranquil woman, not to be disturbed by much. Then I started having little issues with friends and family members out of nowhere. It seemed as if people were picking issues with me and problems with me even though I was already suffering enough. This was the work of that woman. I felt that something was wrong; it just didn't seem to make sense. But finally, after dealing with that for some time, I went to go see a brujo.

"The brujo confirmed to me that it was a woman that my husband was seeing that wanted him for herself. He explained to me that she was working strong spiritual works against me. She couldn't seem to control my husband, so she was attacking me. The brujo told me that the Baron of the Cemetery would help me.

"He could revoke and turn back all the attacks, cleanse, and protect me. So he advised me to meet him on a Friday at the cemetery. There he came with a straw bag, wearing a hat and carrying a bottle of rum. He came in and greeted me and took me over to the cross of Baron. There he pulled out from his bag a cigar, various liquids, a rosary, candles, and a silver bell.

"He lit a candle and put it there in front of the cross of Baron. He began praying and ringing the bell. From there, he started rubbing me and cleaning me with the liquids. His voice changed; he started saying some things I didn't understand. I felt tingling up my arms and legs. Then he started rubbing me with different plants and continued saying things. Now I know that this was a Gede sent to prepare me, but I didn't know that then.

"After he finished, I went home. I felt different—a little dizzy, a little dazed. But I had things to do, so I got on with life and after a few hours I felt fine. That night I dreamt of a man with a long beard standing in the doorway of my house. He took a mantle and tossed it around my shoulders. In return, I gave him a cup of coffee and a peso. He smiled then disappeared. I didn't know much about the Misterios. I had seen it around, you know. I know people who go to brujos. I had consults before. But I was never deeply involved. But I knew that this was San Elias protecting me. The man in my dream looked like him.

"In a few days, my life had returned to normal. Sort of, I mean to say—I was sleeping normally again, my family and friends were getting along with me, and the nervousness had gone. But something was left with me. That was the Misterios. I could feel them. I could feel a peace even deeper than I ever had before. I had peace before, but this time it was stronger, more alive. The best way I could say is that it was like a warm light. I was dreaming more and more regularly. Various things that would occur in my dream would also occur real life. I wanted to return to the brujo, but I was scared of what he would tell me that all of this meant. I wasn't ready for anything. However, after a bit, it had started to grow a little weird. I could feel the presence around me. There were noises. Even the kids said they could feel something from time to time. So I went back in to see the brujo.

"In the consulta, San Miguel came to consult me. San Miguel told me that the treatment had activated my own Misterios. And I was being called to be a servant, a servidora. Being left spiritually open was my way of being called. Sometimes, you don't know the peace you have until you don't have it anymore. But Baron brought it back for me. Dealing with the problems was the way that Baron had brought me to be a servidora. The light I felt inside me was the spiritual force. I would need to begin the process of acquiring my power.

"That's how it started for me. After that, I began doing what needed to be done to start getting ready to be *bautizada*, initiated. I never knew that it was going to bring me here, to be a servidora. But this is what it is, and I am happy to help people the way I have been helped."

Baron is one of the Lwa most commonly known to work with *"las tres manos"* or the three hands. One hand is for good, and one hand is for evil. The third hand is a brujo's secret, which I cannot reveal to you in this book. However, Baron is known to be open to negotiations and working out deals and contracts.

One hand is for the light and one is for the dark. The last hand is a powerful secret of brujo's used for all sorts of lightning-quick magic. Since he works three-handed and he uses one hand for evil, brujos know how to make black magic pacts that can cause the death of an enemy within mere hours or days.

In his role as Death, he is also the commander and chief of the world of the dead and the ancestors. Under his command lies all the spirits of the dead both good and evil. As the ruler of the dead, he has spirits of every variety available to work for him or to be contracted out.

He also may be called upon to send out various dead and other spirits for a number of purposes. Most commonly, the dead are sent against enemies.

Since he controls the dead, Baron is also a healer. He can remove the dead and be called upon to reverse attacks or send the dead back to sender. He can be petitioned to heal all types of physical ailments and illnesses. Controlling life and death, Baron is often approached when someone is about to die in order to "buy more time," making the person live longer.

However, his spirits can be sent to work on love partners as well. In fact, he is very well-known for his capacity to bring back lost lovers as well as separate couples. His powers are often called upon when a cheating husband or wife needs to be stopped. Working with Baron, death can be used to have control in any number of ways.

The dead can be worked with to increase a business or improve its profits. They are great so long as you have them under your control. They're not so great if you don't. This is a tricky business, working with the dead in such a way, that can often go sour.

Raquel's Nine Wild and Out of Control Dead

Raquel was a businesswoman who owned a small boutique. It had been her dream for over a decade and finally it had come true. But by the end of the first year, her business was failing and in debt. No matter how hard she tried the boutique just was not bringing in enough. Not finding any other solution, she sought out spiritual help. Unfortunately, the spiritual worker who assisted her didn't do everything just right for Raquel, and the mess that she came to me with was worse than the one she had started with.

First off, the other brujo gave Raquel nine dead that he grabbed up from the cemetery. The purpose of these dead was to help bring in customers, lift up the business, and get customers to become loyal to the business. As a portal and center for the power of the dead, the brujo set up a special altar for Raquel to maintain the magic. Raquel was given rituals to complete weekly in order to feed and care for the dead and keep them working.

At first, the dead were amazing. Raquel said "it was a miracle" how they were able to turn her business around in a mere matter of a week. Truth was that the boutique had never done this well in a week, even when "it was good." Needless to say, Raquel was overjoyed. She had hope again that all her hard work, sweat, and tears would not go down the drain.

But after about a year of working with the dead, they started to become completely unreliable. Unfortunately for Raquel, she had lost her contacts with the brujo that had set her up. Unable to find him, she did her best to try to get the dead to work again. She increased the rituals. She made more offerings. She did more magic. However, this would work for a day or so, and then everything would go way worse than before. She was getting nowhere and the business was sinking. As if that weren't enough, the dead were now starting to show up in her dreams and make requests and demands. She started having insomnia and fatigue from the lack of sleep, which wasn't helping anything.

Finally, she came in to see me. She was in a terrible state. "I'm not sure I will make it any longer," she said. If the dead were upset, nothing would go right. It was leaking more and more into her home and family life. Feeling ill most days, Raquel was starting to break down. Naturally, when she came, her nerves were a wreck and she looked a hot mess.

Raquel's issue was clear. The dead had overpowered her. Over time and through the many offerings and rituals, the dead had become more powerful than she was. Instead of being her servants, they had become her masters. When she had first received them, she had more power than they did and was able to control them. But they had become terribly effective in the world of men, and their power had grown immensely. Since she was not on the spiritual path, she was not in the process of unraveling her power. She was now completely powerless against them.

"We'll have to dismantle the dead, disconnect them from you, and cleanse you," I told her.

"But I'll lose my business . . . ," Raquel replied with a look of distress. The dead had obviously woven into her mind and obstructed her clarity. She wasn't fully able to see the path that she was headed down, if she continued. They had played on Raquel's greed. With it, they were able to create a strong bond that stopped her from letting them go.

"You'll lose your business the way you're going anyway. Don't be a *tonta* (dummy). We can save the business but not if you play games," I snapped back at her. That is what it took to wake her up, to get her to realize what was truly going on. I could see she was upset at the insult, so I was happy. I knew I was getting through.

"So what are you going to do? Wait till you drop?" I questioned her.

"I have nothing left to lose. If this doesn't work, I don't know. . . . I give up."

"*Callate* (shut up), relax, and lose the nonsense. Baron is going to help you." I wrote out a list of materials she would need to bring to me. We set up three appointments: one for me to check out the boutique, the second to remove the dead, the last to get her luck back and put her on track.

She returned a few days later to pick me up and take me to the shop. As soon as we parked, I saw three of the dead right at the front of the shop. One was in front of the door, the other right inside of it. One was reclining back on the wall in front outside of the shop. The one before the door was menacing and obviously was keeping people away. We noticed each other, and the look upon him told me that he wasn't happy.

As I walked up to the shop, I felt the resistance he had as I walked "through him." Normally, this technique would not be advisable. It is better to have the dead move. But in my lineage, we have the ancient secrets of brujos, which allow us to do this. Unbeknownst to the dead, I was already prepared. By walking through him, I had created a link between us. I would later use this link to work the sacred work.

I walked through the next dead inside, who was a bit friendlier than the last. Keep in mind, however, that I am a brujo. So friendly to me wouldn't necessarily be friendly to you. In the shop, I noticed two more dead. Some were missing in action. Throughout the shop, they had created little nests of negativity. Like rats, there were hidden pockets throughout for them to use and store force whenever they wanted.

Raquel led me back through the shop into the storage room. Here behind several boxes was the altar of the dead. Each dead had a stack of offerings. Behind me was a huge box, the size of a suitcase, filled of old offerings yet to be disposed. This she told me was just a week's worth of offerings and work.

Tossed on my shoulder, I had brought my *macuto* (straw bag) filled with all the items I would need to dismantle the altar and collect the dead. From my bag, I pulled out a white candle, my bell, and my tcha tcha. Next, I took out nine small black bottles and arranged them in a circle. I lit my candle and began calling upon Baron. With bell in one hand and rosary in the other, the prayers and ritual began.

Baron swooped in and a wind came through the shop. A set of wind chimes in the room started playing. At the door of the shop, the bells that were attached played as if someone had entered. Raquel got up to go check—no one. Of course, it was just Baron making himself known.

Now, with the presence of the Great Baron of the Cemetery, we could really call and control all the dead. All of them needed to be present so that I could bring them with me. As each dead responded and came forward, I brought them into my body and placed them into a bottle.

Some of them tried to shake me. Some tried to stir or frighten me. Those that were severely angry used whatever they could to intimidate me. But I found it all quite hilarious, the games they played. Many were "having fun" at Raquel's expense. Some had grown tired, obviously, and wanted out of the deal they had made with Raquel. Each one had his own grudge or issue with the situation. I understood them, as well as Raquel, in their plight. Either way, it mattered not. Into my body each would come, and into the bottle they would go.

Once this part of the ritual concluded, Raquel immediately remarked that the whole shop felt different—lighter—including herself. "We're not done yet," I told her. "We've just touched the surface." I began to dismantle the altar and place each item in various bags. Each bag would be disposed of with respect in another location.

Out of the macuto came an incense burner, incense charcoal, scissors, and a number of different incenses. The pockets of negativity had to be removed, and this would be accomplished by smoking out the entire shop. Then I could start drawing luck back into the shop.

Due to the nature of the incense, we had to open all the doors and windows to the shop as I did the smoking. After getting to every area and cleansing it individually, we quickly shut all the doors and windows to the shop and got out of there. I left the incense pot smoldering in the center of the shop. Now the shop would get a total fumigation. We would return two hours later to air it out and bring in the good. As the shop fumigated, Raquel took me out to lunch.

After lunch, we returned to finish the next phase. The shop was totally clear of all negativity and had a very neutral energy to it. It was neither good nor bad. It was more like "well, it is what it is." This was good, and it was visible that Raquel had become more relaxed this time when she entered her store. Now, we could do the work to bring in all the good luck, clients, and success that Raquel so desperately needed.

First off, we needed to smoke out the shop with incense to draw that luck and prosperity. Plus, the last incense was so stinky, the shop needed it. As I proceeded with other work, various incenses were lit in phases to draw more and more luck.

Then I placed protections at the four corners of the boutique. This would ensure no negativity could successfully attack the poor shop again. These protections were a number of Centinelas given by Baron to protect the shop from all sides, the four directions. These powerful spirits became the guardians of the space and shields.

Now that the shop had become a fortress, I could place the proper puntos of success and attraction into it. One punto would serve to draw the attention and desire of customers. Another would get them to buy and keep coming back. The last would be for success and prosperity to begin to pile up in the shop. These powerful puntos ensured that Raquel would finally get out of this mess.

As for the space where the altar of the dead once stood, I had Raquel wash it down with the appropriate spiritual washes as I was doing my work. Once it was completely physically clean, I set up a small devotional altar to Baron for Raquel. Baron and his Centinelas would now be Raquel's help and make sure her shop succeeded. Lastly, I prepared—which means to empower with power—items for Raquel to use as aftercare on the shop. I left Raquel with instructions for the care of her shop and her altar.

Raquel returned two weeks later. The shop had completely turned around. She was amazed at how things had shifted. She was ready to begin the next section of work that we needed to do to get her right on track again. It was great to see her filled with new hope and some life again. The business succeeding again had reduced her stress immensely, and it was clearly visible.

Children of Baron of the Cemetery

The children of Baron of the Cemetery are usually found to be quiet, introverted, and stable. They tend to have a certain air of aloofness or nonchalance; however, it is not from a sense of superiority. When out of alignment with Baron, though, the children of Baron often suffer from spiritual issues, problems with negative spirits, nervousness, and fear. Attraction or being intensely afraid of death is often normal for those with a strong connection to Baron. Children of Baron are usually easy to get along with, but if their power is not unraveled, they often have issues making deep and lasting connections. Children of Baron are often very introverted, unless the connection to Baron is made and unraveled. During their youth or childhood, they often feel very out of place or awkward. Although this is not uncommon for all children of the Misterios, this is stronger for the children of Baron. It is made even stronger if the person is also meant to be a brujo.

As already noted, Baron is often known to bring people into the tradition. Because of this, often people confuse Baron as being their own particular Misterio.

Baron is served on Mondays and Fridays. In the santuario or altar of the brujo, his space often features a large cross. At times he is represented with a skull. Stones and bricks can be found here as well, which are used in special works to Baron. Baron is often given flowers, a common offering in any cemetery worldwide for the dead. A top hat, a mantle or cloak, machetes, and canes can be found on Baron's altar or among his things as the various tools that the various Barons work with. His altar is always placed on the floor. Another special dish that is made for Baron is one of plantains, sweet potatoes, and other tubers prepared in a special way.

Papa Gede and Los Gedes

The Gedes are the children of Baron and La Barona. There are thousands of Gedes, and they comprise the majority of the Black Division. In the 21 Divisions, there are certain Gedes that are foundational—they form the foundation of the group and run the show. They keep all the other Gedes in line. The Black Division works like a family. They are considered to be a great family of the elevated dead. When a spirit has reached a certain point in its development, Baron and La Barona will rebirth them to the status of Gede. Thus, as Misterios, they become able to continue their paths of unravelment and development of their spirits.

They stand to represent all the different aspects of death and life after death. As humans, we all have a connection to death and therefore to the Gedes to some degree. The Gede is the revival of the spirit on the other side. In the spirit world, he represents the spirit having transitioned and elevated. They come back to help the living attain grace and mercy, as well as achieve our life missions. The Gedes are a reminder that life after death exists. As such, new Gedes spring up regularly as they are reborn into such status.

The Gedes are known to be crude. They cuss, fight, mimic sex, tell dirty jokes, and can be very vulgar. Gedes are above the level of human constructs and social rules. They demonstrate that life need not be so serious all the time. They also show us that what other people think, at the end of the day, doesn't really matter, as we all attain death. They do not need to care about the rules of the living as they are above the realm of the living. As such, they often like to tell embarrassing secrets about people. They especially enjoy watching uptight individuals squirm in embarrassment as their secrets are exposed publicly. With this they demonstrate that secrets can be poisonous and what you see is not always what truly is.

Gedes love to continually talk about sex in all its forms. They regularly speak about genitals and are known to refer to people as genitals. They dance in a very suggestive way mimicking sex. Gedes love to grind and wind their hips. They grind on people and dance with people, often making hilarious exaggerated noises and gestures. This is because the Black Division is concerned with birth, death, and rebirth. They teach that survival—and therefore sex—is important. They say and do things that are often appalling to the living. So when they arrive at a ceremony, you will see the crowd go wild. There will be laughter everywhere, and you'll know one of the Gedes has to be there.

The Gedes are known as powerful protectors of children. Gedes know the importance of children as children are the future and usher in the next generations. Brujos will often call upon one of them to protect a pregnancy. Like children, the Gedes are known to be a bit mischievous. They like to create a little mischief and havoc from time to time. We say that when a child is very hyper or mischievous, it is likely they have a Gede near to them.

Don't let their lack of seriousness fool you, though. The Gedes and the Black Division are incredibly powerful. They hold all the knowledge and wisdom of the dead, death, and the ancestral spirits. They have been here since the beginning of humanity and will continue after its end. It is due to this very fact, that Gedes can see across lifetimes and into the bigger picture, they teach us not to be so serious about what truly doesn't matter. It is their way of reminding us to focus on what is actually important. Due to their ability to truly see and the wisdom they hold, these Misterios are very psychic and skilled in prophecy.

The colors of the Gedes vary; however, the main colors are white, black, and purple—each Gede having his or her particular combination of preferred hues. Like any family, they all have their individual personalities. Also like every family, they also share certain qualities and traits.

A special drink is made for the Gede known as Piman, which is raw white rum in which twenty-one Scotch bonnet peppers have been soaked. Now, Scotch bonnet peppers are some of the hottest peppers in the world. The Gedes will drink this, and they love it. This drink is sometimes used to prove the truth of a Gede's mounting of the horse—to demonstrate that a possession is real. There are many ways in which the drink is used. Sometimes the Gedes will wash their faces with it. Sometimes they put it in their eyes. Other Gedes will wash their genitals. This is a very dangerous drink when someone is not mounted by a Gede. I have seen peoples' throats close up as a result of swallowing it. In one ceremony, a woman pretending to be possessed by a Gede washed her genitals in this mixture. She ran screaming to high heaven because it burned her severely. The Gede possessing me afterward prepared a special mixture to "cool her hot pussy" in so many words.

Most Gedes wear sunglasses. The sunglasses are usually missing one lens. There are actually a few reasons for this. Many say this is so that the Gede can see above and below the ground. Gedes watch both the realms of the living and the dead. Yet, there is another symbolism here as well: It is that the penis only has one hole.

In one ceremony I was at, Papa Gede mounted on a brujo explained it. Sitting on the ground with his food, he was surrounded by the congregation. As he was eating, one of the participants said, "Viejo (old man), why do you only have one lens in your glasses?" Papa Gede hopped up, went up to the person, and pulled the brujo's penis out of his pants. He said, "Look here. How many holes do you see?" The woman responded, "One," and the crowd started laughing. Then Papa Gede began dancing and singing a song about sex.

Most of the Gedes are male. There are some female Gedes, but they are few in number, in comparison to the males. The reason for this is secret. It is something that is revealed to those under apprenticeship with a brujo when they are ready. This is one of the Key Secrets to understanding life and one's life path. Your life path is the road of your being and development—what you do, who you are, whom you connect with, your work, etc. When you are aligned with your life path, your life works smoothly. You are serving your purpose, and you know it. You start to live a life with very little to no friction as you are doing what is meant for you.

The feast of the Black Division and the Gedes is November 2.

Papa Gede: King of the Dice

The most well-known Gede is Papa Gede Limbo Lakwa, often simply referred to as Papa Gede. He is known as the head and leader of all of the Gede Misterios. He is the first son of Baron and will always be seen beside him in a bayi or santuario. Gede Limbo is represented by St. Expedite. Known as San Expedito in Spanish, this fellow is a very famous saint. First off, like Santa Marta (whom you will get to know in another chapter), he is not a holy individual recognized by the Catholic Church. However, he is known worldwide for his capacity to get things done fast. He is often called miraculous for this reason. St. Expedite, like Papa Gede, is known for his power in the realms of finance, money, luck, and work.

He wears a checkerboard or a black shirt and black pants with one leg rolled up to the knee. He keeps a macuto (straw bag) and wears a straw hat. He doesn't like the light and prefers the area to be dimly lit when he arrives in possession. He wears the sunglasses with the lens missing. In his bag, he keeps his money, his tools, and his cards and dice, along with his other implements. He loves white talc, pouring this all over himself and covering his face with it. He will smoke a cigar or two cigarettes at the same time. He uses a walking stick, which, as he puts it, is also his penis. When mounted, he will dance in a very sexual way using the walking stick to represent his cock.

As the first son of Baron, Papa Gede is known to take advantage of his position and status. He is given charge of caring for the dead, especially the fresh dead. He is known for going around town to collect them and bring them back to the cemetery. He can be seen going to various hospitals, funerals, jails, and streets, and collecting the people who have died there. However, it is not uncommon for him to use them to his advantage. He will often send them on tasks, pass his work off to them, and use them as assistants. While they are doing all the work, he is out and having all the fun. He loves to go out to gamble, have sex, and dance.

For this reason, some people describe him as a vagabond. He is always trying to find a way out of doing his work, yet retaining the credit. Although he loves money, he doesn't care to work for it. Instead, he'd rather look for the easiest methods to attain it. This he does by using his charm and capacity to network. He loves to laugh and joke. So, he has an easy time making friends. He knows how to make his money stretch.

One way that he goes about this is to keep some of the fresh dead that he goes to collect and sell them to people as work spirits, puntos, and zombies. This form of zombie is an astral zombie: a spirit who is enslaved to work. It doesn't have a physical body, like what you think of because of books and movies. It's not uncommon to see Papa Gede making deals with people, selling zombies and other muertos (dead), during ceremonies. In fact, he is a great salesman and dealmaker. I've seen him various times walking around announcing, "Zombies for Sale! Zombies for Sale!"

Although Baron knows this is going on, Baron has a huge job to do. At the end of the day, one way or another, Papa Gede gets things done. So Baron, being as patient as he is, never stresses himself out about Papa Gede's antics.

Papa Gede is stingy and doesn't like to share. He doesn't share any of his things, but especially not his food or his money. He is always on the lookout for thieves and the police. Being a bit of a thief and con artist himself, he knows he has to stay on guard. He has a tendency to steal small things from time to time, especially from the other Misterios. He tends to be a bit suspicious of people and their motives. There is one exception, however. He has a soft spot for children and watches over them. He can heal them and is known to give his money for food or to help feed them. Anywhere children need him, Papa Gede is ready to lend a hand.

Papa Gede doesn't care for any form of authority. For this reason, he and the Ogous don't get along. As for the police, he can feel them coming from miles away. It is most common that if he is mounted on one of his caballos and knows the police are coming, he will leave immediately and without warning. There are special protections that a brujo can give on the punto of Papa Gede against the law and the police.

Papa Gede Teaches Some Hard Lessons

You don't have to believe in this tradition, spirits, or magic for it to affect you and your life. Unfortunately, a very commonly held belief is "if I don't believe in it (magic), it can't work on me." That is a huge error and a lesson three individuals were about to learn.

On this day, I had just finished doing a huge removal of a demonic spirit and a cleansing. My client, Janice, had been tormented by this demon for more than two decades. She had been to dozens of various spiritual practitioners to get the situation resolved and dealt with, but with absolutely no relief. This demon had tortured her, causing her misfortune in all of her relationships since college. Naturally, after having done such a huge work, I sent Janice home and took some rest before getting to the remainder of dealing with this entity.

But before I could take a nap, the demon was already making manifestations of its power, showing me that it was there. First, I tried to go into the basement where the ceremony had taken place in order to grab my smokes. When I flipped the switch to turn the light on, it shone out in purple for about ten seconds before bursting into a huge mess—glass everywhere, total darkness. Upon coming upstairs, I heard a huge crash, and I went to look outside. Out on my porch, I saw a storm had brewed outside in that short time made of purple clouds. I stood there in amazement, as I absolutely love lightning and thunderstorms. A three-pronged purple lightning bolt spilled forth. Now, I know that there is purple lightning, but in my whole life, I had never seen it where I lived. It was beautiful and awe-inspiring all at once. As this was going on, a stray black cat came up to me. As I bent over to pet it, it immediately started hissing at me and moving into attack mode. I ran inside and slammed the door just as the cat began to charge me.

Inside I went to the kitchen for some water. The cat came to the kitchen window, meowing and crying. I felt bad for it, assuming it wanted food or out of the storm. As I went into each room, it followed me from window to window, crying profusely at each. So I went to the door once again, this time with some milk. But with the door open, it started hissing at me yet again, acting crazy, and going in for an attack. I said, "Hell with it," and shut the door yet again. If I hadn't lived it myself, I would have thought it was something out of a movie.

At this point, I was exhausted. So I decided to shut out the world and go to sleep, take a good nap. I could deal with all of this once I got up. My nap was interrupted shortly thereafter, however, with people knocking on the door. Opening the door, I saw the storm was still going and three of my friends were there. It was the strangest thing: I hadn't seen these friends in years.

"How did you find me?" was my first response.

"Damn, what a greeting. . . ."

"Your mother told us where you lived."

"Okay, but you can't come in. There is a demon in here, and he is loose. I have to remove him and tie him up before you can come in, so you have to come back in a few hours."

"You're crazy," they said, "we don't believe in that. We believe in God. We can't be harmed."

"Then you can come in at your own risk," I responded.

They came in, and after we chatted for some time, I was informed by Spirit that it was time to cleanse and remove. By this time, my aplasa had returned. She had left when Janice left to go to take care of some of her own business.

I told my friends, "I'm about to call the spirit now, so you can stay in this room and I will come back and then we can hang out then."

I went into the altar to call Papa Gede. This way Papa Gede could come to collect the demon and take him back to the spiritual world. Papa Gede proceeded and did the work that had to be done to collect the demon so that he could return to the spiritual realm. Afterward, he was giving my aplasa instructions on what I needed to do as a part of the cleanup and aftercare.

However, like many individuals who don't believe, my friends didn't listen to me about staying out. They came in to see and speak with Papa Gede.

And Papa Gede, being the dealmaker, was ready to make some deals. Papa Gede always says he knows a fool when he sees one.

So with the eldest of the three, Bernie, he struck a deal: a date with a woman who refused to deal with Bernie at all, in return for three servicios. Bernie believed all he needed was a chance with her to get her to change her mind. With the second, Manny, he agreed to give him "wisdom and discipline" all in return for another servicio. My last friend, Tomas, was a bit more informed. Papa Gede told him so: "You, you know. You already have a dead protecting you." Tomas confessed he had gotten protection from a Palo Mayombe priest (a related Afro-Caribbean religion). Papa Gede continued, "But you need to stop doing what you are doing, as the police are watching you. You will end up in jail and you will lose." Tomas thanked Papa Gede for the advice.

Afterward I returned, and they all told me the story. I tried to explain to Bernie and Manny how gravely serious what they had done was. Making a deal was a huge thing. Tomas was chiming in as I spoke telling them the same. But they wouldn't listen. They hadn't grown up in the tradition as I had, although they all came from families that had practitioners.

Well, Papa Gede made good on his promises. But unfortunately, for them, they didn't make good on theirs. Within less than a week of making the deal, Bernie went on a date with the woman he had been so avidly pursuing. And everything went well—exceedingly so. They ended up getting together and being official, for a little while, that is. Bernie never came back to make good on his promise. The woman broke up with him. He ended up stalking her, and she took out a restraining order on him. He became so obsessed with her that he violated it and was sent to jail. Eventually, he returned to his senses. When he did, he finally came back and told me all of this. He made the servicios that he owed to Papa Gede then.

Manny, on the other hand, was dealt a hard card. Upon his asking for "wisdom and discipline," the Gede warned him that he didn't actually want that, but he insisted. My aplasa also jumped in to warn him, telling him not to ask for such a thing. But he shoved off all advice and told Papa Gede that it was exactly what he wanted. So within two weeks of the agreement, he got into a fight with some other guys. The only way for him to get out of the mess with his family was to agree to go to join the military: wisdom and discipline, indeed.

Lastly, although Tomas was originally in a better position, he didn't escape unscathed. Basically, he didn't listen to the advice given to him. He was selling drugs and continued to do so. He was caught and sent to prison for five years due to the vast number of drugs that he was caught selling.

Papa Gede loves to "tell it as it is," and so he is very blunt. His cussing would put a sailor to shame. He loves to cuss and he loves using swear words. He is loud and lewd. However, he is honest. For this reason, he is known as a great seer and diviner. He will often use his playing cards or dice when prophesying for people. Whether you like how he delivers the message or not, you will know it is true.

He can intercede for you when you are in trouble with the other Misterios. Often, he will be the only one willing to do so. He will also tell you the reason why you are in trouble with the other Misterios. Often, when the Misterios become upset at a servidor, they go silent. They will not explain why they are mad. The servidor is expected to know or to investigate and resolve the issue. Papa Gede, however, can and will often come through and tell the reason for the problem.

Papa Gede is able to help people achieve luck in gambling. People wanting to be professional gamblers seeking real success in gambling often come to brujos seeking Papa Gede's help and favor. In fact, among Papa Gede's tools are dice, playing cards, and money. It's common for him to give out winning lotto numbers. In fact, it's a well-known talent of his.

Brujos are able to prepare someone to be able to dominate games of chance and win repeatedly.

Papa Mario, an elder brujo, explained how this process works.

First, the brujo has to call Papa Gede and get his agreement to do the work to give the person luck for gambling. If he agrees, then you can begin to prepare the person. Papa Gede knows all of the dead even better than Baron. He has more dealings with them. Baron is simply too busy to get to know each and every dead on the same level that Papa Gede is able to. So he knows all of the best dead who are the luckiest and best to play in games of chance. After he agrees, then the brujo checks to make sure that the person has the strength to "carry" the dead upon him. (In essence, the dead will be sitting on top of the person he or she is working for.)

In order to do this, the brujo puts the individual to a number of tests. For example, in one of these tests, the brujo will prepare a grain of salt and place it up on the hand of the individual. Then the individual will be asked to lift the hand. If the person is unable to lift that hand, the weight of the dead will be too much. You see, the dead that is working for the person has to be able to have full control over the person's body while playing. That is how the dead helps the person win: the dead will be the one gambling with the other "living" players.

If the person cannot carry the dead, then the brujo begins the process to prepare the person to be able to do so. This can take up to two years, but it is very worth it. If you can have a dead like this, there is nothing stopping you. You will certainly have lots of money.

In fact, I knew a guy who had a dead like this. One day I will take you to go see him. He was a millionaire at one time, but he lost the dead. Now, he's back here and broke. But he was a professional poker player because of that dead. He had many houses. But when he didn't take care of the dead, the dead messed him up. He spoiled him, too, and now no other dead will work with him that way.

Once the person can pass all the tests to carry the dead, then the brujo can put the dead on him. If you try to do this on someone who can't carry that weight, they will go mad. They will just lose their mind. But if the person can carry it, then you can put the dead on him. Once the dead is on the person, the person will be knocked out for at least three days. They will not wake up, but they are still alive. The dead is taking over what he needs to do his work. When the person finally gets up, the dead will be there. You can see it in their eyes. You see that it is not one who lives there, but two. It is the dead and the person, both in the body.

Over time, the two will blend together more and more. But if you have spiritual sight, you will always be able to see that other shadow that doesn't belong. When you have a dead like this, it is dangerous. It is not for the weak. You cannot be of a weak constitution, because the dead will eat you up over time. Like the guy that the dead spoiled—when you meet him, you will see that he is just a bag of bones. There isn't much left to him. He is weak, and it shows.

But when a man is younger, you know, he can handle it at least for some time. Once the person gets up, he will be up for seven days straight. He will not go to sleep. It is the dead. So happy to be alive again, he won't want to sleep. During that time, the brujo has to feed the person special food so that the dead can "sit down" and become grounded in the person. As the dead calms down and is seated in him, the person will start to come forward more and more. Now that the person is back in control, the brujo can test the dead.

In one of the tests, the brujo hides a special bottle. The person tells him where it is, because the dead tells him. In another test, the brujo asks the dead the location of an aplasa. The dead will respond with the location. After various tests, the person will then be put to go play some practice rounds of cards to see how it goes. All of this is making sure that the dead is working properly. Once he is cleared, the person is free to go gamble and use his new powers to make lots of money.

But—and this is what tripped up the guy I told you about—the person has to feed the dead every so often. He has to go back to the original brujo and get the dead taken care of. Otherwise the dead can get upset, angry, weak, and a whole bunch of things can happen. The other thing is that the more the dead does, the more he has to be taken care of—meaning the more he brings to the person, the more he wants back. In other situations, the dead can grow so strong that he overtakes the person. Then it is the person who is under the dead. Now the dead is running the show. So there are lots of things that the person has to watch out for.

Really the best way of doing that is that after some time, you remove the dead. But a lot of times the dead doesn't want to go. The dead and the person will have become greedy, wasteful. So it won't want to leave. And the brujo can't get rid of it if the person refuses to release it. But also the dead won't want to let the person out of their hands either. Even that can get tricky. If the two have become too intertwined, then the person can die from removing the dead.

Children of Papa Gede

Children of Papa Gede, when connected, elevated, and aligned, are great with money and business. They are excellent communicators and often have big networks. So they are known for their capacity to make great deals that are very advantageous to them. They are also known for their playfulness, general cheer, nonchalance, and laid-back nature. They tend to get along with everyone, although there is often the edge or vibe of a bit of a rebel. They will use this rebelliousness in order to prosper and gain what they want. Often they are very sexual and forward about it. When unelevated, children of Papa Gede are known to be lazy and wasteful. They will suffer from a lack of direction or desire to progress in a stable manner. Not caring what people think, they will often waste time in unproductive activities or avoid work. They will often think they are "getting one over" or in some way "winning" by living in this manner. It's not uncommon for them to get caught up in ways to make fast money, use drugs, and gamble or party excessively. Papa Gede people, in general, do not like or care for authorities or authority figures. They prefer to live on their own terms and, when elevated, don't care about others' opinions.

Santa Marta

Lubana, also known as Metresa Filomena Lubana, is the best known Metresa of the Cemetery. The image of St. Martha the Dominator is used to represent Metresa Lubana, and so she is also known as Santa Marta. St. Martha is the only female saint to have taken on a dragon. She belongs to the Black Division, although she has puntos in other divisions. In some places she is known as Baron's daughter, in others as his concubine.

She is usually visualized as having the form of a huge serpent—sometimes green, but other times black or brown—but she actually has various manifestations. The cemetery grounds are her home. She is a Metresa of the earth and fire. These different puntos display her powers and domains over various realms. Most commonly, however, she loves to mount her horses in her snake form.

When mounted, the horse transforms into a serpent, slowly slithering throughout the room and space. Hissing and flicking the tongue, Marta will traverse the space removing negativity. In this form, she has the capacity to increase people's sexual powers of attraction, especially those of the men in the space. She is also able to open roads and remove all obstacles that lie in one's path. In serpent form, she is unable to speak just as a snake is unable to communicate in human language. So when she is in this form, she communicates telepathically with those whose powers are developed.

In one of these puntos, she manifests as a Metresa. As a Metresa, she takes the form of a half woman, half snake. The upper half of her body will sit up like a cobra, and she will begin to speak. Here she is given her drink and her smokes so that she can relish in them. She will then be able to speak messages and consult. At times, she will also cleanse individuals or give her punto when manifested in this form.

Most well known for her powers of domination, Santa Marta is often seen to be wild and uncontrollable. For this very reason, there is quite a bit of gossip about Santa Marta. Santa Marta is unfortunately often mischaracterized by people both inside and outside of the culture. In certain places, she is worked with to be asked to stay away rather than called upon.

Among her offerings, a special plate is prepared for one of her favorite dishes. This servicio consists of a raw brown egg sitting atop a mound of dry coffee grounds. She loves Malta, which is a molasses drink. Black bitter coffee and red wine are also given to her.

Her sacred day is July 29. Mondays and Tuesdays are her sacred days of the week. On these days, her servidores ask her to clear the paths for the week to come. In the badji, she is kept with Baron and the Black Division, which is her base home. Like all the spirits of the Black Division, she is served on the floor. However, she is also known to have a close relationship with Candelo and can also be found there. Purple and green are her sacred colors, although we also give her red.

Santa Marta and her image have a vast history. To begin with, the image itself is not of a saint at all. Rather it was adopted and came forward to represent the powerful force known as Lubana. The image used to represent Lubana actually comes from an advertisement for a circus performer employed by a German-based circus. It was eventually brought over to Africa, where it was used to represent the African Vodou deity Mami Wata.

In the Dominican Republic, you will hear that Santa Marta comes from Africa. This is because this image was brought over from Africa at some point. In Haiti, you'll hear various opinions. Many say that she is a "Dominican Lwa," and a few recognize her origin in Africa. So, among the Haitian Vodou priests as well as the Haitian caballos, some don't work with her. Instead they refer anyone needing her out to Dominican caballos and brujos.

And yet, I've also seen Haitian as well as Dominican brujos—especially those with darker skin—say that because "she is a black saint" that the opposite is true: that they have a stronger connection. The simple truth is that she is a Misterio. To try to reduce that will only lead to not truly understanding her.

The truth is that everyone's experiences with Lubana are going to be different. She is the type of Misterio who likes what she likes and doesn't like what she doesn't. There is no middle ground for her. She either takes to you or she doesn't. Either way she'll make sure you know it. She doesn't get along with everyone, and there are many tense relationships that surround her.

She can be incredibly entrancing and alluring with her powers of bringing forward sexuality and sensuality. Thus, she is able to "tie up" and control those who come under her spell. Just as she did with the dragon, she is able to win over people and Misterios alike. For some this brings awe, yet for others, fear.

One of Santa Marta's most famous spells is a special oil lamp made to bring back a lover. She loves oil lamps, and this is one of her specialties in magic. She is said to consume the oil as it burns away. Her powerful spells are capable of dominating human and beast alike—lover, friend, or foe.

Santa Marta Drags Him Back

Regina came in to see me because her husband had left her for another woman. Three years and counting, she had tried countless ways to get him back with no success whatsoever. It was a sad case. Not only that, but he wasn't even trying to deal with his children or connect with them in any way. He was living in the home of the other woman, and it seemed like things just continued to grow between the two of them.

Left without any other recourse, Regina found me. After the consultation, I knew exactly what to do and whom to call upon for her. The powerful Metresa Lubana would drag him back. So I gave Regina a list of things I would need her to bring back for me: a dirty sock of his and hers, names and photos of parties involved, any other links of his. Links are items such as hair, dirty clothing, nails, or fluids from the target of a spell. She brought the items to me, and I started Regina's work.

Invoking and sending Santa Marta to work out this issue for Regina, immediately I began to see positive signs on day one. While the work was still in progress—as it was a working that would take nine consecutive days—Regina called me to let me know that he had called her. This was quite a turnaround, considering she hadn't been able to speak with him on the phone for months. She would text him occasionally to let him know about the children, to which he wouldn't even respond. A phone call was crazy.

She said he sounded sheepish. He "just called to say hi and hi to the children." And Regina was superexcited to know what was going on, what was happening with him. So she wanted me to find out, to ask the Misterios and find out for her. However, Santa Marta is Santa Marta, and her response was "What is happening is happening." That's the thing with the Misterios: sometimes the answer you get is just as puzzling as the situation to begin with. Santa Marta doesn't like to be pushed or badgered. She becomes like an angry, hissing snake.

Before the nine days finished, however, he had actually stopped in to her job to see her. That was the beginning of them slowly reinitiating a connection. As you can imagine, there had been many changes throughout the years for both of them. There were lots of things and situations that would need to get sorted in order for them to get back together fully. The children had also suffered significantly, so all these relationships would need healing and time.

Santa Marta Starts a Snake Pit

At this particular ceremony, Santa Marta mounted me and began consulting with the people. However, as Mina reported:

"After she spoke with each person, she would have them stare into her eyes. She would start hissing and swaying. Then the person would start swaying too. She then touched them on the head, and they would fall to the ground, convulsing at first. Then they started slithering across the floor. By the time she spoke with everyone, I was the only person left (not possessed). I was hopping around everyone, totally lost and confused as to what to do.

"Then she said to me, 'You are running in your life like you are now, but in life you can't see all the snakes in your roads so you keep tripping. Slow down. Your body isn't holding up the weight of your head.'

"Then she turned into a snake herself and slithered throughout the room. Slithering over other people who were also like snakes crawling around all over the ground.

"I was scared at that point. I totally didn't know what to do. That's when you finally came back to. And you looked around and started laughing. You looked at me and started laughing at me. Do you remember?"

I shook my head no. I didn't remember. I usually don't remember the first ten to fifteen minutes after a possession.

"Then you popped up from the floor, said some words and stomped your foot. At that moment, everyone's bodies went limp. They all started waking up, looking around, dazed and confused. I walked around helping people off the ground and into chairs.

"Once everyone was seated and had something to drink, I sat and thought about what Santa Marta had told me.

"The first thing that came was that I was trying to run too fast spiritually. I was trying to be more advanced than I was. I could see that clearly, because I was totally lost, confused, and very, very scared when I was the only person left. Like you, Papa, always say, 'A priest can't be stuck with fear.'

"Secondly, in my life, I was tripping left and right. I was trying to advance and yet everything that could go wrong was. Little things, big things—all type of things wouldn't go according to plan.

"Lastly, I totally understood what she meant about my head. I had become very judgmental. I wasn't taking care of my own spiritual practice, and so I was off. But then I was also criticizing everyone else, even to the point of thinking that I was or could do better than others even though I wasn't even doing as much as others. So she definitely made herself very clear to me."

Lubana Gets Rid of the Other Woman

Regina, whom I had helped get back with her ex, was still in a sticky situation. Although Lou had returned to her, he hadn't fully severed ties with the other woman. He was back and forth. Remember, over the years, his relationship with her had become more and more entangled. Making such a switch was not easy or quick. Plus, the other woman didn't want to let him go.

So after some time of having tried to figure things out on her own, Regina was back. She needed our help again in order to get rid of the other woman once and for all. She came back with three large, beautiful purple bouquets for Lubana, just another thank-you for her previous help. She wanted to know if Santa Marta would be willing to help her again. And she was.

This time, I went to the cemetery to perform a special Retiro Spell, or Go Away Spell. This spell would work to disintegrate the ties between Lou and the other woman. He could then be free to move forward with Regina and work things out. In the cemetery, I created a mini fire, which burned brightly as the invocations and the spell were being worked.

In just a few weeks, things had completely fallen to pieces between Lou and the other woman. After the spell, they had begun to fight about even the most trivial things. It was like no matter what they did, they were getting on each other's nerves. There was nothing they could do to help it. In the end, they decided it wasn't working, and Lou returned free and clear back to Regina.

In return, Regina paid her dues to Santa Marta by giving a large Hora Santa. Along with all the usual offerings, the table featured twenty-seven bouquets of purple flowers. Regina is now a very faithful servidora of Santa Marta.

Lubana Heals with a Giant Serpent

My godmother Nancy knew and had great relations with lots of brujos. In fact, whenever we went to Santo Domingo, we had a list of visits to make. We would get in the boat that would bring us over from Puerto Rico, and once in Santo Domingo, one of her many associates would come to receive us.

This time was no different. However, once we were picked up, we went to visit an old friend of Nancy's I had never met before. His name was Lionel, and he was a very tall and fit man. About sixty years old, I would say he looked more like forty. Then again, I was never a great judge of age. His skin was the color of milk chocolate, and he had wide warm brown eyes. Random little white hairs sprinkled throughout his shiny short black hair. His voice was clean and sharp.

Lionel greeted me warmly, offering a seat and a drink of Mama Juana to start the day. Mama Juana is a Dominican cure-all prepared in alcohol with herbs and spices and drunk like a shot.

"Como esta la culebra hoy?" ("How is the snake today?") Nancy roared out with a laugh.

"Which one?" Lionel shot back with a grin.

Apparently, Lionel served Santa Marta in a special way. He had a special serpent—in fact, a huge black serpent—who was served and worked with as a living embodiment of Santa Marta. The snake lived in a huge hole in the ground that was under the shelf of the altar. Next to the altar shelf another table sat. This is where Lionel would work his magic and conduct treatments with the snake. In some of these treatments, he would lay the serpent on the body of the sick person. Just thinking about it gave me the shivers.

Lionel was able to call the snake out of the pit on command. He told me that at certain times of the year, the snake will sleep or rest on the altar itself. To feed the snake, he would place live animals in the room and shut the door. She would come out to feed when she was ready.

As they sat telling me about Lionel's work with the snake, a woman who had been cured by Lionel and his serpent arrived with some cake for him and his household.

She told me that she had been barely able to walk when she finally came to get treatment from Lionel. "I knew of Lionel and had heard of his treatments. I know others who had been cured by him. But I also knew that he cured with the snake, and I was scared to death. But it came to the point where nothing was working and my mother begged me to come to Lionel.

"When he called the snake and I saw it, my eyes went huge. I started gasping, 'It's huge.' I thought I might die right then. Then when he brought it to me, I started screaming."

At this point, Lionel went on to imitate what happened and this lady's screams. Nancy joined in the fun, acting as Lionel. Merrily they acted it out, screaming and laughing like children. They were so animated, that at first the lady thought it was funny too, but you could see she was growing embarrassed.

"Oh, don't be like that. . . ." Nancy said as she saw the lady's embarrassment. "It's no big deal; you're not the only one to react like that."

The lady then continued, "So he then laid the snake on me and began praying. It was slithering all over me, touching me with its tongue. But he was directing it with a stick. It wrapped around my legs—first one then the other. This went on for long."

She ended up coming in for multiple treatments, each time becoming more and more at ease with the serpent. One day Lionel told her, "After this (treatment) you'll be completely cured." And indeed, she was. After that, she came to love and appreciate the snake.

"She saved me: Santa Marta, the snake, and Lionel. I wouldn't be here in front of you like this without the serpent. I am forever in debt to them." Ever since, she's been bringing gifts to Lionel, Santa Marta, and the serpent.

It's a Small World After All: Lionel and the Serpent

I was hanging out with my goddaughter Milady when her friend from work Lucia stopped by for a visit. After introducing me as her godfather, she sat with us for some coffee. All my godchildren know that I love an afternoon coffee. Lucia was a short, heavy-set woman with warm chocolate skin. Sporting a short hairstyle, she had a very harsh, almost manly voice.

"I'm so happy to finally meet you," said Lucia. "Milady is always speaking about you and your eyes; they're amazing. But you look familiar. Do I know you? Have I met you before?"

"Not that I remember," I responded.

"So you are a brujo? 'Cause you don't look like one."

I smiled devilishly. "Appearances are deceiving," I responded.

"That's so true," she said, laughing. "I'm very familiar with brujos. My family always went to brujos, and there was a big one where I lived. He worked with Santa Marta, but he did so with a huge serpent. Have you ever seen anything like that?"

My eyes lit up. Could it be Lionel? Responding by simply widening my eyes, I listened as she continued. . . .

"He had a huge black snake. I know lots of people he cured with that snake, and he had helped my brother get work with that snake. I always wondered how he did it. But snakes creep me out," she said quivering. "And I'm scared. Santa Marta, she's intense. I'm scared of her, but that is the one he worked with. You know her right?"

"Of course, what brujo doesn't know Santa Marta? She's over there in the cemetery."

"Exactly, what do you say about her? Is she bad? 'Cause I heard some things about her. Some people say she is bad."

"That's people's gossip! She is not bad; she is just very direct! People love to talk nonsense, especially about what they don't know."

"True," she replied as she turned to Milady, saying, "Oh my God, Milady, you didn't tell me that your godfather was so handsome."

"You make lots of sense. . . ." she continued on at me. I listened to her go on about different spiritual topics for some time. Then asked, "Was the brujo's name Lionel?"

"You know him?" She looked at me astonished. "How do you know him?"

I went on to tell her how I used to visit him with my god-mother Nancy. It turned out her mother knew Nancy as well as a few other people that I knew. So we went on talking, catching up on old news, at which point she told me that Lionel had passed away. Just a few months back.

"And the snake?" I asked, curious to know what became of it.

"It disappeared, and no one has seen it since Lionel passed," she told me. Yes, it's a small world after all, I thought.

Santa Marta's Children

Her children are very passionate with strong characters. Santa Marta's children are very forward and obvious about who they are and what they are about. Although a good quality, this can also bring them problems at times. Santa Marta's children are also very strong, generally speaking, not just in character, but also physically and emotionally. When unelevated, this can lead to anger, problems with people, and frustration. They have a dominant nature about them and have issues with control. It's common for her children to be mischaracterized by others, due to the dominating energy. Her children are loyal, like her, but they will punish and take out their anger on those who have been disloyal.

Division Legba/Legba Division

The Division Legba is the group of Misterios connected with doors, passageways, and gates. Doors, gateways, and roads all represent opportunity and the potential for growth and progress in the 21 Divisions. When one has one's doors or roads closed, this denotes that they lack any chances, opportunities, and therefore luck. Obstacles on one's roads lead to troubles and issues. This division is the one in charge of opening the doors and roads in order for progress and success. Likewise it controls closing the doors and roads so that negativity cannot reach the servidor. This most well-known Misterio of this division is its leader, Papa Legba.

Papa Legba

Papa Legba is the spirit who controls the doors and gates. He is the guardian of the Threshold and chooses what and who will pass through. He is one of the first to be saluted as we ask that he open the gates between the spiritual and material worlds. No spirit or person can pass without his permission. As such, in some lineages, he is seen as the leader of the 21 Divisions.

He is seen as a homeless old man who wanders the streets. He wears burlap rags and uses crutches as he limps around. In some places, he is given a walking cane instead. A hunchback, Papa Legba asks for charity from those who pass him by, blessing those generous souls who see his value even though he lacks money. This is also the way that he will manifest when he mounts a horse. At that time, we will also give him a straw hat to wear, along with some red wine, rum, or hot chocolate to drink. He is then given a cigar that he will puff on contentedly. He also carries a straw bag, known as a macuto, in which he keeps the few items he owns.

In the badji, Papa Legba is seen as St. Anthony of Padua. His color is brown and his sacred day the 13th of June. There brujos will give him his servicios, which can include coffee, red wine, rum, bread, hot chocolate, and chocolate. He loves to smoke a pipe with his tobacco or is given cigars. His macuto will be there, along with some of his symbols, keys, or a cross. However, there are a number of Legba, as Legba is the family name of this group of spirits.

Papa Legba originated as a major deity among many of the African tribes who were brought to the New World in slavery. There and in Dominican Voodoo, he is a spirit of the Crossroads, doors, and passageways. He is also a spirit of fertility and as such has dominion over children. He protects them and helps people conceive. In many of his servicios, the feeding of children is central to making a service and offering to Papa Legba. With such a deep relationship to children, it is no surprise that he is connected with all the Lwases Marassa (children Lwa).

Papa Legba Helps Angela Conceive

Angela was forty-eight years old when she came in to see the Misterios and get help.

"I haven't been able to conceive for more than five years. Before I was with my current man, it wasn't a problem. I already have two grown boys. But he didn't have any and wanted to have them with me. And I wanted to give them to him. We tried for five years with nothing. We couldn't afford in vitro.

"My friend sent me to you after you had gotten her husband out of a legal problem. So I came on a day you were consulting people with the Misterios.

"That day it was El Viejo San Miguel doing the consultation. This wasn't the first time I had gone to try to get help spiritually. So, I was a little familiar with people getting mounted, though not with the Misterios.

"So that day I met San Miguel. Your cousin was your aplasa that day, Daniela. She brought me in and sat me down. San Miguel shook my hand, gave me a look over, and he immediately said, 'Your womb is blocked and so you can't have the child you want.'

"I was shocked, to say the least. It sent shivers down my spine. In fact, look (pointing to her arm). It gives me goosebumps just talking about it.

"Then he told me a few more things. He told me that I would need the help of Papa Legba and that I would have to bring you certain things. He told me I would have to devote my baby to Papa Legba in order to get his help. I promised to name the baby after him in some way.

"I brought you the items. You did whatever you did with them, though I didn't understand how you were going to make it work.

"Why is that?

"Because I guess I expected different. I thought you were going to give me a spiritual bath or something to take. Do something like that. But you just took the items and did what you did. I remember thinking, 'Will this work?'

"Then a week later you called and told me you were done. I remember asking you what I needed to do, and you said, 'Have sex, get pregnant, and don't forget that you need to bring for the offerings once you're pregnant and keep your promises.'

"I did as you said, and it was about a month and some change later when I got pregnant. From then I did what I had to do, fulfilling my promises to Papa Legba. When I had my baby, it was a girl and I gave her the middle name of Antonia. As you know, I've been very, very devoted to him ever since. I love him so much."

Papa Legba is very common among the Misterios who bring people onto the spiritual path. This is totally understandable, with him being the cosmic gatekeeper between the spiritual and physical realms. Many people who have not grown up in the culture now find themselves in the 21 Divisions because of him.

Papa Legba opens the gates to spiritual truth and light. He has the power to grab the attention of every person, as he is tied with all people to some degree or another. I receive countless emails, letters, correspondences, and experiences in which people tell me that Legba brought them onto the path.

Papa Legba is one of the most approachable Misterios. He is also very visible. Many people have seen or had experiences with him. He can show up as an old man at the crossroads, a beggar, a homeless person of wisdom, a "devil"—in fact he has many faces. "Legba has as many faces as there are souls," my Aunt Nancy would say. There are, in fact, numerous Legbases or Misterios named Legba, which form up the family. All of them are generically referred to as Papa Legba, although each actually has his individual name.

In Dominican Voodoo, the homeless are blessed and hold a special power. Since they don't own anything and lack possessions, they cannot be cursed. They also have the capacity to give blessings and the blessings of Papa Legba in particular. Papa Legba has been known to manifest as "a crazy disheveled-looking homeless person who speaks knowledge" and can even give out winning lotto numbers. This is not uncommon. He can also deliver messages of warning through them. Papa Legba teaches about humility and generosity. He also holds the sacred teachings of gratitude.

He is also a trickster. He is well known for this. He is known for making deals at the crossroads. Many people revere him, but just as many fear him. For as a trickster, he works to bring about Divine balance. One of the ways he does so is through confusion, misdirection, and creation of chaos. By stirring things up and getting people off center, he teaches how to find true centering and balance.

Papa Legba is often referred to as being miraculous for his immense power. As mentioned, all spirits must get his permission to pass through the gates for what will or will not manifest on the physical world or in the spiritual world. If he bars the way, it doesn't matter what a person or spirit does, it will not come into being.

As the patron of doors and gateways, he knows where everything is and where it has gone. He has the capacity to bring back lost people, things, and situations. For example, brujos know how to invoke him to retrieve a lost lover or a lost job. But he can also tell a brujo where to locate an item that has been lost.

Papa Legba really enjoys food and eating. His services and offerings always feature plenty of food in abundance and the generous giving and sharing of it. In this way, Papa Legba teaches about flow in life—the truth about giving and taking, which brings balance.

Papa Legba has a wife, known as Rosita Legba. She supports him in all his undertakings and keeps things in order for him. Papa Legba is known to have a very mercurial disposition, which means that he is "going where the wind takes him," which is part of his magic. Therefore, Rosita has to keep things in order and organized for him.

The power of Papa Legba is that he can produce such swift and quick changes simply by shifting whether a door is open or shut.

Papa Legba Heals Doris's Foot

Doris became a believer and devoted to the Misterios after having received a healing from Papa Legba.

"I came to a ceremony with a friend. I don't remember which ceremony, uh . . . let me think . . . I am pretty sure it was a ceremony you were doing for Gede. Anyways, I came here with my friend, you know, to kind of support her in dealing with these things (spiritual matters). I have had readings before and little things, but I wasn't really into these things. That day, we came here to your house and I sat in the basement, like in the corner, because I didn't want to get in the way. I didn't come here for me, ya know, so . . . but then one of your godchildren, a Mambo, got mounted by Papa Legba. He was walking around, you know, talking to people. I remember he had a crutch, and he had his face covered with a hat. You all had also put a brown robe on her; it looked like a monk's robe. Eventually he made his way over to me. He actually pushed past two people who were standing in front of me. I was sitting on a chair, so I was down, behind them. Really you couldn't see me from where he was at. But he pushed past all those people and he said, 'You! You foot is bad, it has a . . .' and made a sign with his fingers. I knew what he meant immediately. I had been dealing with bad bone spurs and other foot problems for some years. So I nodded yes. He said, 'Let me see dat foot' and pulled on the leg that had the problems. Someone brought him a chair, and he sat down, pulled off my shoe, and sprayed my foot with rum, I think. Then he blew smoke. He asked for something that was in a bottle; it looked like greenish-brown liquid. He rubbed that on my foot and massaged it all in deep. He took a good long time working on my foot. Then he put my foot down. That's when he told me that I needed that stuff (an herbal preparation) from you and to keep rubbing that in there. Then he left and went to speak to other people. But immediately my foot, which was in pain, was in less pain. It had subsided. I would say that before he began it was like an 8 but by the time he finished it was like a 2 or 3. I remember that very clearly and that is why I was so much in a rush for you to get me the bottle (of herbal preparation) to use. Since then I used it like you told me, and it has gone down, down, down. Most days I don't even feel anything anymore. Every once in a while, it may bother me—especially if the weather is wrong or bad. But most days, I don't feel anything at all. Ever since then, I've become very much a believer in Papa Legba. I don't know much or about everything, but I do believe in Papa Legba."

The Road Is Long!

In Dominican Voodoo, Papa Legba owns the crossroads, where any two roads cut through each other. The journey of life is known as the great road. As a result, in life, your roads can be opened, closed, blocked, prosperous, blessed. In fact, it can have a multitude of states. Spiritually speaking, your "roads" relate to your opportunities and options or lack thereof. Bad luck and a lack of good luck are often a result of closed roads. As the keeper of the roads, Papa Legba is involved when someone is suffering from such conditions.

Life has its ups and downs. Basically, its fluctuations are normal to some degree. However, when your roads are all closed, you have no opportunities or options. You are stuck in your situations and problems with no way out. This can and often does lead to other problems, which arise from stagnation. Spiritual people work toward keeping their roads opened, clear, and blessed. This takes maintenance and effort. However, things also happen in life that can close up the path for you even if you're doing maintenance.

Papa Legba Triples Clients and Business

Oscar was barely able to make ends meet. He was a private practice attorney, and two years before, things had suddenly shut down for him. His once-thriving practice became just a shell of its former glory. In fact, in the two years he even sold his home. It just wasn't sustainable.

Oscar found me online after having searched "far and wide" for help and not being able to turn things around. Even after having hired a number of "spiritualists and psychics" to help him, it had all been for nothing.

The truth was evident right from the beginning. His roads had been closed by two different forces: One was a woman who was scorned and cast her spell on him. The second was a small group of competitors, who were cliqued up in a conspiracy against all those who were not in their group. Between both of these attacks coming at him, Oscar was being shut down.

Papa Legba came forward as the solution. We would need to clear, clean, and open Oscar's roads. After that, I could draw in the good luck, financial success, and prosperity Oscar so desperately needed.

Just a few days after the working, Oscar reported having gotten "four new clients all on the same day." A few weeks later Oscar emailed saying:

"After those few clients, about a week later, I closed a few more clients. It has been growing like this ever since. I have been taking care of Papa (Legba) as you told me, and I bought a little table for his statue. I got my secretary back and I'm talking to a lawyer friend about teaming up with me because the caseloads are getting bigger, but I don't want to turn anything away. . . ."

Children of Papa Legba

Children of Papa Legba are often very jovial and upbeat people, when elevated. They tend to have a comedic side to them and are nonchalant and relaxed in their way of being. They tend to be very much a "go with the flow" type of character, especially when it comes to fun or having a good time. Papa Legba people usually have a very high energy, which can at times be seen as being hyper or overactive. They have a tendency toward excitability. They also love to be with people, but prefer to "walk alone" or without a crew. Papa Legba's children are generally quite proud and self-confident. When unelevated, the children of Papa Legba often become cranky and greedy. They are known to hoard and will tend to push others away from them. Likewise, when unelevated, they will be insecure, overly proud and arrogant, but sometimes feigning humility at the same time.

Division del Fuego/Fire Division

This division is comprised of all the Misterios of Fire. This division's ruler is known as Candelo Cedife and is associated with St. Charles Borromeo. The Fire Division is also known as Division Candelo (Candelo's Division). The color of this division is red. It is mostly consulted for reversing hexes, getting revenge or justice, resolving difficult cases, cleansing, protection, and improving business and work. The Fire Division is one of the largest within the 21 Divisions. Within the Fire Division, many smaller divisions also exist.

Candelo Cedife: Leader of the Fire Division

Candelo is visualized as an older black man with salt and pepper hair and a short beard. He is old, so he's also known as Papa or *El Viejo* (the Old Man) Candelo. Just like an old man, Papa Candelo loves the warmth and hates the cold. He is strict, wise, humble, and compassionate. He is also a spirit who makes few demands and is straightforward and simple to approach. His number-one demands are honor and respect.

Papa Candelo has seven puntos. These are each different manifestations of Candelo. However, the central punto and most common is Candelo Cedife. It is he who is the leader of the Fire Division. *Cedife* is Kreyol for "Is Fire." Candelo is the literal manifestation of the Mystery of Fire. Candelo's fame and popularity are very widespread. In Puerto Rico, he is known to work with the dead, a Baron in his own right.

Papa Candelo is identified with St. Charles Borromeo, whose image is used to represent him. He is also represented by a popular votive statue or image of an elderly shirtless black man, wearing red, black, or white pants and sitting cross-legged. At times, a pipe is in his mouth. Brujos give him a machete, which is one of his main tools. He is often also given a cauldron or pot in order to make his fires, which he uses to heal and do his spiritual work.

Candelo enjoys cock fighting. He is known to carry a magically enchanted red rooster. When he isn't working, he likes to go to the local cock fight and play a few rounds. The magic of his rooster is that everyone underestimates it. People see the rooster and think it is too scrawny to win, not strong enough. But that is solely a part of the enchantment; the other part makes it so that Candelo's rooster wins every time.

He also loves his women and to drink. Candelo is known to be a bit of a womanizer and a player. But he always goes back home to his wife, Candelina. He can be very smooth with the ladies and is known to have strong passion.

He is one of the Lwa that I have had many, many interactions with. He owns many heads, just as he owned my own Madrina's head. He is wise and serious, and when he speaks, he knows exactly what he is talking about. Thus, he speaks very matter-of-factly. Wherever he goes, he demands respect. He is the Lwa of discipline and acts as the disciplinarian to make sure the traditions and work are being respected and done properly. Thus, he has the capacity to close off a brujo's connections to even his Head Misterio and shut down his powers if he is not following the codes.

Candelo is very devout and protective of his devotees. Those who seriously follow the codes and are children of Candelo, and he will protect them from all sorts of evil and harm. He doesn't tolerate people going after his children in any way and is known to be vengeful. His child doesn't have to ask for him to be vengeful; it is just his way. After protecting his child, he will go in to seek justice on behalf of his child.

Brujos serve Candelo with red candles, yellow rum, and cigars. When he arrives in possession, he will tie his head with his red fula. He then proceeds to take three candles and pass various parts of his body through the fire. He may then proceed to shut the flames off in his mouth, eating the fire. Once he has seated himself comfortably, he will take his cigar and begin smoking as he drinks his tafia, or rum. He speaks with a heavy accent as he dispenses valuable advice and warnings. He doesn't become angry easily; however, he doesn't tolerate any form of disrespect. He expects seriousness, especially in the spiritual work.

Candelo is known as a healer and respected for his powerful capacity to cure the sick. He is very well-versed in medicine and the magic of herbs, which he uses for his healings, as well as applications of fire and heat to cure illness and disease.

Candelo bestows protection. He also gives protection to children and is known for his love of them. He loves for a fire of Florida Water to be built, and then he will walk through it, stamping it out. At times, he may decide to light his hands with Florida Water and cleanse people with it. He is good for uncrossing those who have been hexed. It is very common for him to apply these treatments during Manis, Prilles, and other ceremonies as well as when he is consulting in the altar.

At one Mani that I held, a woman had brought in her two-day-old grandchild, a beautiful baby girl to be given protection by Papa Candelo. Papa Candelo held the child up, looked upon her, said the sacred words, and presented the child as he does when bestowing his protection. Two days later, the grandmother returned, telling me that El Viejo Candelo had already looked after the child. She proceeded to tell me how the day after receiving the protection, the baby girl was supposed to go with her aunt to see her other grandmother. But that day, something happened that rearranged all the plans. So the aunt couldn't pick up the baby. Later on that same day, the aunt got into a terrible car accident. Had the baby been with her, it is likely she would have died. The woman came to ask me what she could give me to present to him in thanks.

Candelo is known as a premier businessman. Not only does he keep an excellent, successful, and prosperous business, but he has great public relations skills. He understands how to get along well with people. As strict as he is, he is still known to have a strong sense of humor. He grasps how to put life in perspective and things in check for his followers. For this reason, people come to him when they need a boost in business. But this is most significant in businesses that rely upon customer interaction, sales, and services. He can bring you a boost in business very easily. In fact, it is known that he can turn your business upside down or right side up in less than a week when a brujo invokes him on your behalf.

As leader of the Fire Division, Candelo has many connections to all the Chiefs of the Divisions and many other spirits. Candelo and Belie hold a very close relationship, as best friends, and can often be seen working with each other. Together, they also assist in dominating evil and enemies of the brujo and his clients. They work to bring about swift justice and punishment. As discussed above, in some lineages, he and the Baron of the Cemetery are considered to be one and the same. He is known to have a spicy relationship with Santa Marta, and they are known for working together in domination. He is the godfather of Anaisa Pye and about the only one who can really keep her in line—well, as much as one can in the case of Anaisa, that is. He works with La Gunguna to compel men (or women) fulfill promises made when they were in love. His connections are endless.

Candelo Cures Xenaida

Xenaida came to see the bruja Nancy because she was terribly ill. She was falling apart at the seams, and nothing seemed to cure her. See, the issue was that she wasn't absorbing any nutrition, so slowly she was literally disappearing. She was a walking bag of skin and bones.

When she came in to see Nancy, it happened to be on a Tuesday, when Nancy normally called Candelo to come and consult her clients and help those in need. So when Xenaida came in to the bruja's waiting room, Candelo was already there in the bayi. He was in the midst of consulting another woman who was experiencing issues with her son in school.

Xenaida had come with her mother, because she was no longer in any condition to drive. Due to malnutrition, Xenaida often felt strong waves of sleepiness and total exhaustion, being wiped clean of all energy. So her mother came in with her and to support her in this process.

When Xenaida came into the room, Candelo looked at her and told her that she was already more than halfway in the cemetery. Xenaida was at death's door. In fact, her body was shutting down. It was already in the process of fading.

Immediately, he sent one of his assistants to fetch some herbs. Quickly tearing the herbs and mixing them with various oils and liquids, he made invocations. He was mumbling over the herbs, with a lit cigar hanging out of his mouth as he worked his magic into them. Suddenly, the mixture was set ablaze. Candelo started picking up handfuls of the burning magic mixture and pressing and rubbing Xenaida's body and joints with it.

Xenaida felt a surge of energy run through her. It was the best she had felt in years. But as quickly as it came, it left. She felt a little down, but within minutes came three more surges of energy. She felt suddenly alive again. He was bringing the light and force back into her body.

Candelo proceeded to tell Xenaida's mother that Xenaida would need to come in weekly for treatments until she was cured. He then began to prescribe a very set and specific diet that she would need to follow to heal and support her healing process. Candelo made it very clear that he held the mother responsible for Xenaida following this diet.

Week by week, Xenaida received treatment. By the end of three months, Xenaida was eating regular food like a normal person. She had gained a significant amount of weight back and was getting back to work. Although not yet at 100 percent, she was more than 80 percent of the way. Within a few short weeks after that, Xenaida says she was back functioning "better than she had ever been" and was working toward making up for lost time.

The Children of Candelo

The children of Candelo are known to be like him: loyal, wise, and strong. They can at times be stubborn or bullheaded, but they tend to be honest and true. What you see is what you get with a child of Candelo. The men may also be a bit of a womanizer, like Papa Candelo, but the same can't be said of the women who are very serious when it comes to relationships. Do not betray someone who is the child of Papa Candelo, as you will wish you hadn't. Papa Candelo's children can be quick to anger and becoming frustrated or upset. Candelo's children are generally hard workers.

Candelina Cedife

Candelina Cedife is Candelo's wife. Represented by Our Lady of Candlemas, known as Candelaria in Spanish. Her feast day is February 2.

Candelina is a tranquil, yet serious and strict Metresa. Her energy is controlled, but she is very no-nonsense. She is not super-prissy and feminine like some of the other Metresas, but cannot classify as a tomboy. She is elegant but tough and quick to act. She will call you out, in a nice, yet firm manner. But being with her husband at the head of the Fire Division and a Fire Division Misterio herself, she can be easily made upset and grow enraged.

She enjoys everything in red. She loves sweet red wine and anisette. But what she really enjoys is smoking cigarettes and thin cigars.

She is not concerned with love and sex as they connect with many of the other Metresas. Candelina tends to be more interested in the protection of children, protection of the home, steady work and employment, and stability of the family. She sets the rules and discipline of the home. She is associated with new mothers and babies. She is known for her ability to bestow powerful protection upon babies like her husband. In my family lineage, the brujos would bless babies and bestow the protection of Candelina upon them for a donation of two dollars and two white candles on February 2. This is considered the most powerful day to receive a protection for a newborn.

Candelina as protectress of the household is held in high regard for her capacity to dispel and remove negative energy and evil spirits from the home and from people. With her sacred fires, she burns away all negativity and its hold on its victims and brings the light. She is capable of destroying even the most evil and strong connections that are harmful. But in order to approach Candelina in this way, the victim must be totally clean and free of all wrongdoing in the situation.

Candelito Cedife

Candelito Cedife is associated with the Child of Prague, also known as Nino de Praga in Spanish. Like the rest of the Fire Division, his color is red. He is seen as a small boy of about five to six years old. He is known to be a bit on the mischievous side and very close to his mother Candelina. Like many of these Misterios, he is very protective over those devoted to him, and he will help mothers who need assistance with their children. He will help a mother rein in a wayward child when she has no other recourse.

He rarely shows up in possession, but when he does, he is going to try to get away with everything—especially if there are no Elder Misterios around. He will smoke, eat tons of candy, and be rude to the guests. He can also be a bit of a bully. But if another Misterio shows up, he cleans up his act right away. He will pretend as if he is the best-behaved child in the world. He, like his sister, can be a bit dangerous because he is known to have temper tantrums when he doesn't get his way. But he is more controlled, easier to calm down, and thus less temperamental than Candelita.

He is known for his amazing capacity to get people out of jail quickly—even if they are guilty. This is because he can be swayed with bribes. However, because of his temperamental attitude, he can also cause things to fall through and put the person right back into jail. He can be voracious and have a huge appetite that is hard to keep satisfied.

Because of his nature, he is usually left to the brujos to work with. He is not considered safe for someone who is a servidor or devoto to work with. When someone has Candelito with them, the Padrino or Madrina of the person will instruct the person to work with him in certain ways that are safe. This person will also be taught how to handle him by the brujo under which he or she is apprenticing.

Candelita Cedife

Candelita Cedife is a powerful Misterio; don't let her kind and innocent image fool you. She is seen as a young, blonde, light-skinned girl child of about two to three years old. Her image is known as "La Nina de la Espina" or the "Child of the Thorn" in which a small female child is attempting to pull a thorn out of her foot. This is not a saint image at all, but a classical painting that was adopted and became used to represent this Misterio.

Don't let her small size trick you: she is incredibly powerful and actually known to be very dangerous. Working with her can bring fame, fortune, and incredible amounts of success. But she has a very strict way of how she wants things done and how the person who works with her must live.

Candelita is tempestuous. She is known for her wild, turbulent, and stormy nature. She is very jealous and possessive over those who serve her. In fact, she doesn't like children, especially female children. She is known to harm the children of the household if she is served within a home with children, especially if she feels that she is not being treated as the primary and the queen.

For this reason, she is not usually served within households with children, although her image may be kept for protection, as she is also known to have an incredible power to protect. In the instances when she must be served and there are small children in the home, her altar space will be set up in a special and specific way outside. When properly prepared, she will not be able to enter the house and cause disturbances.

She is the child of Candelo and Candelina. However, Candelita was raised by Metresili and Ogou Balendyo. As such, she displays many of the same characteristics as Metresili. She enjoys feminine perfumes, jewelry, makeup, desserts, and sweets. She is also coquettish, very feminine, and delicate. Like Metresili, she is very connected to her emotions, and her emotions dictate her actions.

How did she end up with Metresili and Ogou Balendyo? Well, what happened was that Candelina, who is not very feminine and had been used to being around all men, didn't know what to do with her beautiful child Candelita. But there were definitely issues and friction going on between them from day one. She could feel it. As the child came to grow, Candelina and Candelita just kept bumping heads and having issues. She couldn't understand Candelita and her needs, and Candelita would then throw incredible tantrums. Metresili was wanting a girl child to dote on and dress up. She was upset that she couldn't have one. Upon hearing this, Candelina offered to let Metresili raise Candelita as her own. Metresili agreed and so Candelita grew up with Metresili.

Chango

Chango is very well-known and popular within the majority of Afro-Caribbean traditions. His service and following are huge wherever these survived.

In the 21 Divisions, Santa Barbara serves to represent the Misterio known as Chango. With Chango's help we can over-come that which seems impossible. We can go to Chango when we are facing very strong opposition and can be sure that he will aid us in our mission. Chango is a spirit of protection, of magic, and of wealth. He can assist us in any battle as he is a very strong warrior. As a spirit of luck, wealth, and prosperity, Chango Macho is often petitioned for help in business, employment, and gambling luck. The feast day of Santa Barbara is December 4, and so, by extension it is also Chango's.

In addition to Santa Barbara, another image is popularly used to represent Chango: an African king surrounded by treasure and bedecked with jewels. This image, known as *Chango Macho*, is used by the brujo to invoke this powerful punto of Chango in order to help his clients acquire wealth, gold, and prosperity. Chango is said to once have been a king in Africa, and this image represents that aspect of Chango as wealthy monarch.

He is also known to have a punto in the Black Division. Here he works powerful magic with the spirits of the dead.

While present in the 21 Divisions, Papa Chango doesn't have or hold the same place that he does in many other Caribbean spiritual traditions. This is also true in Haiti. However, there are still some lineages in which his presence and importance are still very central.

I learned that this was because at one time, Papa Chango did hold the stronger position within Dominican Voodoo than he does in many other Caribbean spiritual traditions. However, in the Dominican Republic, the slave masters noticed the slaves' deep devotion to Santa Barbara, who is associated with Papa Chango. At that time, Papa Chango was the leader of the Fire Division. They also noticed that in the slaves' devotion to Santa Barbara, many African elements were still very strongly present. So the Catholic Church, officials, and other political powers made a concentrated effort to eliminate the devotion to Santa Barbara. Remnants of devotion to Santa Barbara remain visible all over the Dominican Republic. You will find many monuments, buildings, and other such areas named after her.

When they came to get rid of the devotion to Santa Barbara and Chango, Papa Candelo arose to fill the void. Between him, the Ogou Division, and Belie Belcan, they took over many of the roles that Papa Chango once held.

In the 21 Divisions, Papa Chango is the lover of Oya, and it is due to her that he no longer walks with the Ogounes. You see, Ogou Balendyo fell in love with Oya. Oya, being a warrior queen, was attractive to Ogou Balendyo, who was constantly out in the battlefield. But, as is well known, Ogou Balendyo falls in love quickly, though often superficially. Oya wasn't interested in Balendyo, but had been trying to rein Chango in forever because Chango loves dancing and women. He is a sort of Casanova with the ladies and loves anyone in a skirt.

Naturally Oya tried everything, but nothing worked. She knew that Chango really loved her, and she was his number one. But she also knew he couldn't commit or keep it in his pants.

So when Balendyo came around, she saw her opportunity to get what she wanted from Chango. She played along with Balendyo, seducing him further and beginning a fling with him. Now, she knew that when Chango found out he would become jealous and possessive. She would then have her chance to make her demands. If he wanted her, he had to commit and stop playing games.

Ogou Balendyo didn't know any of this at first. He hadn't a clue that Oya and Chango had been longtime lovers. Chango, Balendyo's brother, served in Balendyo's army as a general. He was known for his ingenuity and his terrifying nature in battle. He was incredibly vicious and frightening when in the heat of war. But then Balendyo learned the truth.

When Balendyo began planning his attack on Chango, Oya happened to overhear the conversation. Worried that Chango would be taken by surprise and killed, she ran to inform him. But she couldn't find him. As usual, they had recently fought and hadn't spoken in some time. By the time she caught up with him, it was mere minutes before the attack. He hadn't even the chance to get ready.

As the Ogounes and their entire army descended upon them, Oya took up arms to fight with and save Chango. They were able to decimate a large part of the army—just the two of them—and escape. Realizing Oya's betrayal and true love for Chango enraged Balendyo. So he chased them around for a long time, but they always escaped. After some time of this, Balendyo cooled off and got over it. He stopped chasing and harassing them.

Now, Chango throughout this time had been pretty much faithful to Oya and just her. Their relationship grew incredibly close. Oya was happy. But after Ogou Balendyo let it go, Chango went back to his old, womanizing ways. Although upset, Oya realized that no matter how hard she tried, he would always be how he is. Nevertheless, they still fight with each other regularly. Due to the long time spent together, Chango does it less than he used to, and that's good enough for him.

Olisa Bayi

Protector of the bayi and santuarios, brujos place his punto at the entrance of the bayi. From here Olisa Bayi stands guard over the sacred space. Sometimes his punto is put at the entrance of the house instead. He assures that no other brujo is able to bring in magic to harm.

Olisa assists Candelo in making sure the brujo is doing right and following proper codes and protocols. He is seen as a powerful Papa Boko himself. He has a great knowledge of plants and how to use them in magical baths. He is a great warrior and carries a sword, which he uses to cut evil and protect. He is also connected and sometimes served with the Ogou Division, the Division of Warriors.

Division de Ogounes/ Ogou Division

The Division de Ogounes consists of a family of warrior Misterios whose surname is Ogou or Ogoun. This family of spirits comes from the Yoruba slaves, which are also known as Nago. So this division is also known as Division Nago. All of them use a machete, their sacred weapon to battle, and protect and conquer on behalf of their servidores. The owners of iron and metal, they are spirits of war and also connected with the police, military, government, and politics.

Ogou Balendyo

Ogou Balendyo is the warrior par excellence among the Misterios of the 21 Divisions. He is said to come down from the Mount of Olives to fight wars and battles on behalf of his children. When he does, he rides his white horse, ready to give a hand to the downtrodden and heal the sick. Ogou Balendyo is not only a warrior, but also a doctor and healer. As a healer, he can cure instantly and uses his hands as his primary tools. He is an older male about sixty years of age, who has the wisdom of having fought many battles.

He is also the leader of the Ogou Division or Division of Warriors. This division is mostly male and, as you can expect among warriors, a very rowdy and rambunctious bunch. But all of them regard Ogou Balendyo with all honor, never disrespecting him, his rank, or command, as they know that the negative consequences will be severe.

When he mounts a horse of the Misterios, he demands a great deal of respect and silence. He speaks in tones that are just barely audible. And at times he shakes, just like an elderly man. He will be given his red wine in a glass and a lit cigar. Once he has these along with his fula, he will be ready to advise the person or consult. He doesn't stay for very long, although he will stay longer when conducting a healing. Ogou Balendyo is a workhorse, meaning he is constantly active and therefore will often complain of being tired. But off he will run to work and war again.

In the badji, the brujo represents Ogou Balendyo with the Catholic Saint James the Greater. On his altar, you will find the machete, which is his primary weapon. His colors are navy blue and white, though he is also given red. He drinks red wine and is particularly fond of a brand known as *Caballo Blanco*, White Horse, just like the one he rides. He also loves to smoke fine cigars.

He is the husband of Metresili, and together they represent the ideal and balanced couple. Ogou Balendyo is a father figure, very strict and traditional in every way. He is known to be gentle and protective, but can be overly severe. With Ogou Balendyo, there is "only one right way"—which happens to be his way. He is willing to fight in order to make sure that it is known.

Ofelia Balendyo is his closest sister and confidant.

Naturally, many *resguardos* or protections are prepared on the punto of Balendyo. Resguardos can be made as general protections or to safeguard against certain dangers. Naturally, the more specific the protection, the better it is at guarding against any negativity, attack, or harm that may come via that manner.

Ogou Balendyo is the Misterio who set up the *reglas*: the rules that are the standards of practice and tradition. These contain the secrets of proper structure, order, and service that make the spiritual work smooth and effective.

Ogou Feray or Fegay

Ogou Feray, or Fegay, is the sergeant of the Ogounes. He is the type of sergeant who fights side by side with his warriors. His favorite thing to do is fight. He loves war for war's sake. Therefore, among the Ogounes, he is also the premier assassin. His colors are blood red, green, and black. He carries a machete like most of the other Ogounes.

He can be seen in the image of San Santiago, as the warrior in full armor riding the horse behind Balendyo. Feray is more savage than his brothers. He is hotter, more fiery in his temperament, yet he is superprotective and fatherly to his devotees. He expects military precision and diligence. He is very militant and by the book. Feray loves order.

Papa Feray gifted me with a sacred stone when I was only twelve years old. This stone called to me from a dream, which led me directly to discover it in real life. The stone is quite heavy, about the size of a baby watermelon. It's completely black and sometimes becomes shiny, sweats, and moves. I have been honored with the task of being the keeper of this sacred piece.

Interestingly enough, I've been homeless at various times in my life. But no matter where life took me, my sacred duty to the Misterios has been clear. As such, on one occasion I had to leave this stone in a forest I was unfamiliar with in the middle of the night. (Yeah, it's a long story and, if God allows, I'll get to tell you someday.) When I attained a new residence, my first stop had to be the forest to retrieve Feray's sacred stone. So after telling Feray that I was going to get the stone, I entered the forest and the stone called me right to it. On another occasion, having left the stone "stored" in the cemetery, I later came to find it in a whole different part of the burial grounds. The stone drew me directly to it, and without even realizing it, I had sat near a grave to pray and, when I opened my eyes, the stone was before me.

Feray works, and he works hard and endlessly. He works without food or rest. He often doesn't even realize how much he has done as he moves effectively from one task to another. At one time a woman came to me, because she had constant financial and professional issues. Nothing ever came easy for her or even stayed stable. The solution was to give her Feray's punto as was instructed in consultation with the Misterios. The punto in this instance had to be given in the woods and a sacrifice had to be made. In the middle of the ceremony, two police came riding down the road in the forest. At that moment, I told Feray to shield us and make us unseen, as they would certainly disturb the rituals. Sure enough, although the cops looked in the woods and I could even see their eyes, they didn't spot us and kept riding by. Needless to say, my client received her ceremony and has never had another problem with work since. That was in 1996.

When Papa Feray laughs, it's very dangerous because it means he's severely angry. It's terrifying, as you know there will be very bad consequences, possibly even death. His punishments are extreme. Although he usually comes off roaring angry, this means things are good. When he asks his servants to do something, he is fair and gives more than ample time. However, once the time has run out, it's out!

Ogou Badagris

Ogou Badagris walks in Petro, meaning he also walks in that division. In fact, he can often be found by Ezili Danto in the badji. Here you'll find him represented by Saint George. He is the diplomat and politician among the Ogounes. Not only does he confer powerful protection, he can nullify negative energy and poisons.

The three Ogounes Balendyo, Feray, and Badagris form a powerful triad invoked for spiritual battles and wars, destruction of enemies, separations, and extremely powerful protections. Together they can create powerful lightning and thunderstorms.

I was at the home of a fellow brujo and friend, Jeremie, waiting for him to finish his day's consultations so that we could go to the market, pick up supplies, and set up for ceremonies we were doing the next day. I had brought four people from the United States to the Dominican Republic to undergo various spiritual treatments. Jeremie lived in a tiny little country town that was set in the middle of the woods. The closest larger town was San Luis, which was still about a twenty-minute ride out by motorcycle. In fact, the way that we found Jeremie's home was to ask for directions from anyone, as instructed by Jeremy, in the main road for his house. We were told to ride down the street until we passed two houses, a mango tree, and then we would find his house with a huge avocado tree set before it.

We sat on the porch as we waited. There on the porch sat an old washing machine and three chairs. His mother, who lived with him, brought us some fresh shots of espresso as we passed the time. I caught up with her and what had been going on. In the background, you could hear spiritual music from a tape deck blasting loudly. Clients shuffled in and out, and the living room was already packed with people waiting. Many of them had come all the way from the capital of Santo Domingo to receive his help.

Suddenly there was a stir. The Lwa who was in the altar room, Ti Jean, requested a yellow soda be retrieved and set in the sun for him to do a magical working. He then sent someone to get me to come to him at the altar.

I entered the badji. It was a narrow room, like a small train car. Along the long wall opposite of the door, a long table that went from one end to the other. The table had a beautiful green mantle and all sorts of bottles of various drinks, potions, and other infusions scattered across it. Images of the different Misterios adorned the wall. Jeremie, mounted by Ti Jean, sat on a rocking chair at the opposite end of the room. He had a fula tied around his head and another on his arm. White talc covered his face as he puffed a cigar, relishing it.

We greeted each other, and he then told me that he had another Misterio that wanted to speak with me. Ti Jean left and Ogou Badagris entered.

Again greeting him, I gave him his drink, cigar, and fula. He told me that he had been waiting for me. We then spoke about the relationship between myself and the brujo and what we would do to attend the patients. He then gave me a blessing to keep money flowing, which I thanked him for. He then told me that "I just wanted to see you on this part of the land because I always see you on the other side. I am blessing all of the undertakings upon this journey and protecting you."

This was a beautiful statement. Unknown to the brujo Jeremie at that time was that I was initiated in Haiti and the main Misterio there that I would interact with was Ogou Badagris. So naturally, I saw him most often "on the other side of the land," meaning in Haiti. From there he left and Jeremie returned to himself.

Ogou Panama

Ogou Panama takes his name from the straw hat he wears, known as a Panama hat. He is a "country" Ogou and an amazing dancer. Like most of the other Ogou, he is a very hard worker. He both clears the land to prepare it for sowing as well as harvests the grains when the growing is done. Panama is generally a jovial Ogou and also has the knowledge of plants and herbal treatments.

I've witnessed Panama come through at one ceremony to directly speak on some of the injustices he had seen being done, back and forth, by the people there. It was now starting to affect the community overall, and something had to be done. A just Misterio, he listened to a bit of what each side had to say and then set out the ruling. Each party would have to "give an Hora Santa to clear themselves" of the negativity they had caused.

Ogou Neg

Sometimes called Negue, Ogou Neg is a guy's guy. He is strength and known to be quite hot. He is of a wilder nature and so are his methods of war. He doesn't arrive through possession frequently, but he does communicate via dreams and visions. He can be seen living in the woods. He also is known to frequently show up and communicate on behalf of the other Ogounes, without making any mention or reference to himself.

Ogou Batala

Father of the Ogounes, Ogou Batala has the wisdom of a mature and noble warrior. He is stern yet understanding, but very strict. He can be seen in the image of Saint Martin of Tours. He is visualized as being very old and riding a horse. He doesn't come in possession often, but if he does arrive, it is something serious.

Although there are many other Ogounes, these form the foundation of this division of Misterios.

Division Metresas/ Metresa Division

The Division Metresas is the group that contains all of the female Mysteries. All of the female Misterios are known as Metresas. Although all of the Metresas belong to this division, many of the Metresas also belong to other divisions. There are many Metresas in this division, so we will only cover a few of the major ones. Many of the other Metresas we will cover in the other divisions where they mainly find their homes.

Metresili: Leader of the Metresas Division

Metresili, also spelled Metres Ezili, is the "Jefa" or Chief of the Metresas Division as the home of all the female Misterios. Metresili is the spirit of beauty and femininity. She is represented by the image of Our Lady of Sorrows, also known as the Mater Dolorosa.

Metresili is visualized as a rich, light-skinned, upper-class Spanish woman. Always perfectly poised and refined, she is known for her impeccable manners and enjoys life among the high-class society. She loves to get dressed up and attend balls and other fancy affairs. We say she rides around in a white limousine.

Metresili owns a small jewelry business. She keeps this business, not out of need, but rather as a hobby. She doesn't attend the business daily; she has employees for that. Most of the time she can be found at home or out with friends at some function or another. She enjoys a lavish lifestyle, where she takes frequent naps, lovely day trips, and all the best the world has to offer.

She is bedecked in the finest clothing and jewelry. Many of her most precious pieces came from Spain directly. She lives in a beautiful white mansion, where she has many servants to attend to her every need. She owns various other properties as well, which she loves to visit and vacation at. She is known to be very precise and demanding. Her nature is to be very exact.

Metresili is the Misterio of abundance, wealth, luck, and romance. She is the spirit of everything that is luxurious. Very traditional in her ways and lifestyle, she is a very proud Misterio and always makes sure she "looks right."

Her favorite colors are pink, light blue, and white.

When a Mani or other ceremonies in which she is to be honored are done, she requires that she be the first one in attendance. She will be the first spirit to arrive through the caballo. If she feels disrespected by having had another Misterio arrive before her, you will find that she will delay her arrival or not attend at all.

As the spirit of purity and cleanliness, she has a high standard for them in order for her to respond. Many of the Misterios are served with alcohol, cigars, and cigarettes, which Metresili absolutely hates. She sees these as being dirty and stinky. She finds foul smells repulsive, and she will refuse to come wherever there is dirtiness.

When she arrives, she requires that a white sheet or rug be placed for her to walk upon. She hates touching the ground, which she sees as dirty, and thus walks only upon the sheet. A special wash is made in order for anyone who desires to speak to her to wash their hands. This wash contains lots of perfume to make sure the person smells good before they go to approach her. A special greeting is given to the Metresa with the pinky fingers.

Typically, she is very choosy about the individuals she chooses to take possession of. Special rituals and preparations are conducted by her horses in order to increase their chances of receiving her. Along with these rituals, she requires sexual abstinence for a period prior to the ritual. She always prefers to mount her children over those horses who are children of other Misterios.

Being a powerful psychic, she will prophesize and foretell the future. However, she cannot be bothered to consult individuals when she is mounting a caballo. Rather, she chooses to enjoy the service and attention that is being given to her. She will often speak on the miseries that exist in the world and the problems that are plaguing human lives.

Metresili will often end up crying. At times she enters crying, and at others she leaves the possession crying. As the spirit of love, she is also the spirit of sorrow. She feels the pain and suffering that people are dealing with, and this moves her into deep sadness.

Her sacred day is Thursday, and she prefers to be served on her day. Ogoun Balendyo, her husband, will often be found on the altar near to her. She loves all types of sweets and is fond of cakes, desserts, and all that is luxurious in taste. She is often given red soda, lemonade, or sweet juices. She also loves milk and coconut milk.

Offerings that are sacred to her are exquisite and expensive—the best perfumes, powders, and makeups or gold jewelry, chains, necklaces, and rings. Just like in the image of Mater Dolorosa, Metresili, as the spirit of abundance and wealth, loves to be smothered in the finest jewelry that a caballo can give her. Many of her caballos will also keep special clothing for her to wear when she arrives. Along with that, she prefers that her horses keep a mirror, a basin, towels, and soap for her.

When she mounts someone, it isn't usually for a long time. She doesn't really enjoy being embodied in someone as much as other Misterios. Rather, she often prefers to be in the spiritual form affecting and directing everything from afar. Her force is gentle and subtle.

Her husband, Ogoun Balendyo, takes care of providing this lifestyle for Metresili, but he is frequently away at war. This is one of the points of Metresili's sadness. She also knows that he has relations with other women when he is away. But nothing she does can stop it. She had reined it in before, but it backfired.

Metresili is the elder sister of Anaisa. But these two can't stand each other's ways. Metresili doesn't like how Anaisa behaves and interacts with men. To her, Anaisa is vulgar, brash, and promiscuous. She feels that Anaisa doesn't carry herself like a lady. Anaisa, on the other hand, feels Metresili is too serious, stuck up, and a bore. They will work together at times, and yet at others they bicker.

Anaisa, being a powerful witch renowned for her gifts of seduction and sensuality, is known for her ability to attract and control men. One day, Metresili and Anaisa were talking, and Metresili was extremely upset about not being able to control Ogou Balendyo. Metresili confessed to Anaisa that, no matter how hard she tried, she just couldn't stop him from having relations with other women. She was tired of it and was at a total loss. Anaisa, being the queen of gossip, drama, and fun, questioned Metresili more and more, getting all the juicy details.

After gathering all the information, Anaisa told her sister, "I have a powerful trabajo that will tie Balendyo to you forever. He may still deal with other women, but he will never leave you for them. He will always come back to you."

Metresili knew her sister far too well and responded by asking Anaisa what she wanted in return for the magic. Anaisa replied, "Your respect." Anaisa had grown tired of dealing with Metresili constantly looking down on her. Being the Misterio of joy, Anaisa constantly felt Metresili's lack of respect was a buzzkill. Metresili agreed to her terms.

So Anaisa worked her magic. And of course, it succeeded. But knowing Metresili to be fickle, Anaisa put in her own twist. After getting some semen from Metresili required to do the magic, she kept some for herself to keep Balendyo enchanted. Having had the magic done and all being well, Metresili all too quickly forgot her promise. As usual, upon the next event of their meeting, Metresili treated Anaisa with her usual attitude. At that point, Anaisa decided to use all that she had gathered to get back at her sister. So casting the enchantment, Anaisa set up a meeting with Ogou Balendyo.

In that meeting, Anaisa seduced Ogou Balendyo with her powers. She dangled herself before him like a carrot, but just like the horse, he never got a bite. However, during that time, Anaisa revealed to Balendyo all of the secrets that Metresili had shared with her about his infidelities and affairs. Ogou Balendyo, as the type to always be seen as a righteous and upstanding figure, was embarrassed and enraged to hear all of this. But due to the spell Anaisa had cast on Metresili's behalf, he couldn't hold it against her. It mattered not to Anaisa, though, because she knew she had seeded problems between them that would spring up over and over.

Also having connected with Balendyo and earning his trust during this meeting, Anaisa found herself with yet another powerful ally she could control to get her desires met. Ever since that day, Balendyo has remained infatuated and enchanted by Anaisa. Due to this and to her loyalty to him in telling him what Metresili had said, he will do anything to help her when she makes requests. His infatuation with Anaisa is just another bone of contention between him and Belie Belcan, Anaisa's actual husband. Metresili, on the other hand, believes that Anaisa already had sexual relations with her husband, even though Anaisa has explained many times that it never happened. This further cemented her view of Anaisa and yet also stirs up jealousy.

Ever since, this has been the underlying problem between the two sisters. They will work together when they have to. They will tolerate each other. But each one gets under the other's skin.

Metresili Gets Jealous

Metresili loves to be the center of attention. One of the things about her is that when she wants something, she just can't stand seeing anyone else have it. As the mistress of love, she herself loves to receive the attention of men and is known for falling in and out of love with them quickly.

Metresili doesn't care for women, whom she sees as competition in getting attention. Metresili never lacks in male suitors. In fact, when you see her at a Mani, she will be quickly surrounded by the men. As she is the queen of the feminine Mysteries, they seek her favor so that they can progress in love and wealth. Every man knows, if Metresili favors him, so will women.

At this particular ceremony, one of the initiates arrived with a new boyfriend, Damian. They happened to show up shortly before the Metresili portion of the ceremony. Once Metresili arrived, she quickly scanned the room. Immediately she noticed the guy, whom she claimed as hers. Jennifer, the servidora who brought him, took him forward to speak with Metresili who was beckoning him.

"He belongs to me . . . ," Metresili quickly proclaimed.

Damian was shocked. Really, he didn't know what was going on. So he was totally unsure of what to say or do.

"I'm his luck. He has to come serve me, and you need to give me a servicio in order to deal with him," she told Jennifer, who then explained this to Damian. At first, he rejected the idea and was even a bit perturbed by it. A spirit owning him?

But then Metresili gave him a piercing look in the eyes as she stated, "I am your luck. You run in the streets (selling drugs), and you should have been inside (in jail) many times. But every time, it is I who nudges you to leave the place right before they (the police) come. It is because of me that women buy you these (pointing to his clothes) and you successfully live off of them (the women). I have been near to you; I have been the light that has helped you and led you. I have brought you here. You've disrespected me, and each time I drop you to the ground and leave you with nothing, and it is I who builds you back up. Don't think you are just so smart . . . it is not your intelligence: it is me."

He knew exactly what she was talking about. Entranced by her eyes, all he could do is nod.

"So, you will bring me what I ask. You will give servicios here (pointing to the badji) for me. For you lack responsibility, and if you were to keep me (have an altar), you would fail and I would turn on you. And if she wants to deal with you (pointing at Jennifer), she pays me. Same with other women. For when you get too close to them, I pull them away because I am first, second, and last. They can be third. Understood?"

He nodded in agreement. She touched his forehead, blessing him. At that moment, he passed out.

Upon his awakening, she was gone, and the ceremony was back in progress. Later on, when asked what happened, he said, "When she touched me, I felt a white light in my head and a rush of love, a warm rush into my heart, and I couldn't stay up."

Jennifer was jealous. She didn't like it. Damian belonged to her. So when he asked her to come make the offerings, she gave a million and one excuses as to why she couldn't do it. How she would, but hadn't gotten to it yet, etc.

So within just two weeks they had split up. At that point, recognizing the influence of Metresili, Jennifer came to make the offering. Metresili responded quickly, "It's not enough anymore for your disrespect. To get him back, ask the horse what you need to bring me."

So Jennifer was told and brought what was needed. The offering made, Damian who had completely disappeared after the breakup came back within a matter of days. At that point, Jennifer knew she had to bring him to make offerings to Metresili. So immediately she took him to go shopping for the queen.

He bought three dozen of the finest roses, and had them dusted with shimmering glitter, along with chocolates and sweets. As the time went by, he grew to know, understand, and follow Metresili more and more. The results were that his life started to change in a positive way, eventually leading him to the point of receiving the Mystical Marriage with Metresili. Now that he knows who his Lwa is and has gotten on the path, his life has a whole different flavor.

But don't let all the sweetness fool you. Metresili is both gentle and fierce. She is known to carry a dagger behind her at all times for when she needs to protect herself. Some people say this is the dagger that is seen in her heart. She is known for her fierce protection to those who are devoted to her. Her power to dispel evil and negativity just by her mere presence is well known as nothing negative can stand to be around something so pure.

Metresili the Queen of Drug Dealers

As the owner of all that is luxury, all that is expensive and excessive, Metresili is also the owner of drugs and thus a protectress of drug dealers. Drugs are considered luxury items, for if you don't have the means to live and survive, you don't have the means to get high. Drug dealers often live a life of fast money, luxury and abundance. As the saying goes, "Drugs sell themselves," meaning it's easy work in the drug business. All you have to do is let the right people know you have what you have. But living such a fast and dangerous lifestyle has its costs—namely, the coffin, jail, or illness. There are just innumerable dangers to those taking part in this business.

Quite naturally then, this is the realm of Metresili. This often comes as a shock to many, considering her love for purity. But one must also remember that she is also the patroness of deep sorrow, and sorrow often leads to drugs.

Metresili has the magnificent power of being able to protect drug dealers and those who are hiding from the law. Not only this, but she is also the patroness of easy money and even easier work. She can help the drug dealer become incredibly successful in his venture. With her connections to Ogou Balendyo and the law, she has the power to keep those under her protection clear of jail, the sword, or the gun. She demands in return a strict and high level of devotion. As such—as every drug dealer should also know—"you don't get high on your own supply." Dealers protected by her are not allowed to do any of the drugs themselves. She requires a pure mind and body in order to be under her aegis.

Robert was a longtime drug dealer I met at my Madrina's house. He had been coming to her for more than ten years to be protected from the law but also to defend himself from the competition.

"Other dudes were constantly jealous of me. People would try to set me up, and the cops constantly picked on me. That is when I met Mami here (talking about Nancy). She watches over me. She protects me with my Metresili (pointing to the sky). I had a friend who used to come to Ma here for the same thing. One day, we were talking about some shit I was in with the cops, and he asked me, 'If I tell you something, are you going to think I'm crazy?' Nah, I told him. I am not going to think nothing about it, you're like my only friend. So, he said to me, 'I go to a witch, she is this Spanish lady, and I think she can help you.'

"Immediately, I asked him, 'What I got to do?' I was at the end of it, I didn't know what else to do and was tired of all this. I couldn't afford to end up in jail again, understand me, son?"

I shook my head letting him know I understood full well.

"So that's when he brought me here, a few days later. I think, like two days. And what happened? She looked at me and told me all my shit. I knew Tedd, my friend, hadn't told her nothing. It was crazy. I had always believed in God. I believed in ghosts, even though I never saw one. But a lot of people in my family had said they had seen ghosts before. So I believed. I believed in Jesus, of course. And I knew there were angels. But Ma, she is an angel here on the earth."

Laughing at this uproariously, Nancy punched him in the arm playfully saying, "Now, don't you insult me. . . ."

"So she told me my saint was Metresili. She told me what to get, what I had to do, to come back here, and she had to get the court thing fixed first. Then she would bless me with my santa (my saint). From there, I could begin the path. Then I can be protected and I can come out on top. Ma, she is a warrior. That's why I love her so much, because she told me very clearly 'Hijo, we are going to get you out of this shit,' and she did. Just like that.

"I went to court and everything got dropped. They couldn't find the papers they needed. It was good for me. Immediately I came back here to Ma. I brought her flowers, wine, candles, and cigars because she and Papa Chango protected me. I had to give him what was his. I had to bring Ma something too. So when I came here, I asked to take her to eat. But she was tired cause she had worked (spiritual work) during the day. So she asked me to bring her something from the bodega. We sat together and ate it together.

"Ever since, Ma and Metresili, they are my mothers; Papa Chango, my father. I love him so much because he protects and watches over Ma. I love them all. But these are the ones I know. So now, I always check in with them about making any major decisions. But I also bring all my women here for Ma to give them a look over and give them the okay."

Metresili Gets Rid of a Child

Metresili wants to always be perceived as forever young. She is known to have children, although she likes to hide them. Because of her sympathy, many individuals approach Metresili when they are unable to keep a child. When someone needs to abort a child for whatever reason, Metresili can do it for them spiritually, although this comes at a great cost and loss. Nothing that one does is without its repercussions.

Alissa was just starting to get her life straightened out again. She had been utterly destroyed by her addiction to drugs for more than a decade. But through the intervention of the spirit, she was able to not only get off of drugs but also start turning things around for herself. She had been caught up in some really hard drugs and had a hell of a time getting free of them.

But finally, she was clean—and she had been clean for a year. Unfortunately, she had entangled herself with a man who was no good for her. Not only were things getting out of hand as far as the relationship was concerned, but it was already starting to affect her life. Too add to the mayhem, she had accidentally gotten pregnant—although she found out later that the guy had purposefully set things up to get her pregnant to tie her up into a life with him. He was attempting to attach himself to her as a parasite.

Upon realizing that she was pregnant, Alissa was absolutely devastated. How could this happen to her? She had taken all the precautions. But she was further along than expected. Now, Alissa had been serving the Misterios for some time. In a fit and knowing Metresili held the power to have her miscarry, she decided to begin a servicio asking for exactly that favor. It was only three days into the servicio, in the middle of the night, when Alissa felt deep pangs in her womb. Running to the bathroom, she found the bleeding had begun.

Alissa was losing lots of blood—more than expected. So she had to get a ride to the hospital. There she was told that she lost the child. They helped her through the process. This whole thing became a terrible experience for Alissa. "I thought it was going to be much easier and smoother," she said. "I didn't think it would affect me this much. As I was sleeping that night, I was thinking of asking to cancel my request when I woke up. I didn't think she (Metresili) was going to respond to me this quickly. So I still thought I had time.

"On the first night when I did the work, I felt a response from the Misterios saying, 'If you do this, you are not going to have any more children. Are you sure?' And I was like, 'Yeah, I'm sure. I don't care. I just know that I don't want a kid, not with him, and I don't want another kid in my life anyway.' And I was angry; I said it angry. And I felt something, like a very severe energy respond to me, like 'Okay.'

"I should have stopped then, but I didn't. I was on a rampage. Now I regret it. I knew I would never get pregnant again."

The Misterios are powerful forces and they can help you for good or for ill. The forces themselves are not responsible for what you do with them. All actions have reactions and reactions upon reactions. This is the natural law. Alissa, now unable to have children again, is experiencing the natural results of her actions.

Metresili Pays the Bills

I had a situation in which I was suddenly out of a place but quickly found a new one. This new apartment wasn't necessarily any better, but at least it was mine and what I could find right away. However, the electricity was still in the landlord's name, and he was refusing to change it over to mine. He also wasn't paying it. So my lights were about to be cut off. There was no heat in my house, and it was the middle of January. As if that weren't enough, a winter blizzard was building up.

Now, back in those days, whenever a brujo moved a long distance it was a whole process. There is a time in which everything has to be reconfigured. Your badji and altar are taken down. There are rituals and ceremonies that go with that. And it all has to be moved to the new location. This was before cell phones, which meant you needed to have a new landline installed in your new location. At that time, it was also not as easy to carry your phone number to your new location.

If you've never had a telephone landline installed back then, well let me tell you, it was a pain in the rear end, at least where I lived. It took two weeks to get an appointment. Then you would wait around all day, until maybe the person actually showed up. Hopefully, everything was right in the home to get you set up and going right then. If the telephone company didn't make the appointment, not only did they not let you know, you had to ring them and set up for a new appointment, which again might take two weeks.

Once that all got done, then you could finally contact all your clients and let everyone know your new location. Well, I was in the midst of spiritual development, which means that, of course, it took five weeks for me to finally have my phone installed. Periods of spiritual development are often marked by upheaval, mayhem, and craziness just so you know. And that is exactly what was going on for me.

So needless to say, with all the emergencies, the move-in costs, money to live, etc., I was broke. All I had for my Misterios was a single white candle. I offered it to Metresili and told her I needed the money to pay my bills and survive. I promised her that if she got me out of this mess, I would have an Hora Santa in her honor. She was my last hope and only solution. If I ended up in the street, I would have nowhere to go. I reminded the spirits, "If I end up in the street, so do you!"

After closing out my service, I went and laid down to sleep. I was still a little worried, but it was slowly dissipating. I could feel the warmth and strength of my Misterios oozing into the worry space. It is in these great moments of struggle and problems, that we find our biggest growth and beauty.

In the middle of the night I was awakened by a noise. Then I heard a woman's voice that said, "Put on your shoes and go outside. Walk to the right and stay on the street. Keep your eyes to the ground and pay attention; your answer is waiting for you. Hurry up!"

So I did exactly that. After going about three blocks, I saw a paper bag on the ground. Inside of me, I knew that this was what I was sent for. So I grabbed it and ran home. When I got home, I opened up the bag. Guess what was in it? Over $3,300—enough to pay my bills and then have the servicio for Metresili I promised her. That gave me enough time to get things together for myself.

Metresili and the Misterios didn't delay in helping me. So you can bet yourself, I made no delays in getting together what was needed for the Hora Santa. I didn't have my phone yet, so I set myself up at the payphone after the snow had disappeared. There with a folding chair, I sat and made my calls to get this ceremony together. That payphone was mine for the month. And on the day of the party, I set someone up to sit at it, so they could take any calls from people needing directions. If you don't know me, nothing stops me from serving the Misterios.

My house was bare. But I had managed to get the electric switched over. So we had lights. I had also gotten some electric heaters to help with the fact that this old house was absolutely freezing. The altar was the only thing in the living room right when you entered, along with a mattress and the few personal items that were all I owned. My belongings were actually about a trash bag full of clothing and care items. But all of the "empty" space was filled with something: Spirit and my love for it.

The morning of the festivities the house was abuzz with commotion. Tons of people were coming in and out to help me prepare for the beautiful ritual that was to take place. Before the main altar, I had set up a table, consisting of two cinder blocks with a cleaned wooden board laying across them. The table was dressed beautifully by my aplasa Paula with layers of white cloth and lace materials. In the center, a vase of water was featured with a floating rose candle. Flowers adorned the whole back of the altar, and the main altar had its own flowers and candles. A beautiful mani on a golden tray was to the left of the water. To the right, a huge round cake decorated with pink and yellow flowers. The floor, having been washed down with sacred perfumed waters, was now filled with plates of offerings before the ceremonial table. Huge bottles of perfume decorated the front of the table along with the Jarro Divisional and the tcha tcha. Sprinkled about were offerings others had brought for all of the various Misterios.

That evening the ceremony began; the space slowly filling with people. We started with the sacred prayers to get the ritual going. By the time we were through, the house was packed with people. Over one hundred folks had packed themselves into my home. Viviana served as my aplasa for the ceremony. Reina, Dee, and Griselda assisted in keeping things in flow. With this little crew, we managed a beautiful ceremony in which the Divine was honored, spirits fed and pleased, and many blessings given. The spirits illuminated people and brought forward healing. The congregation was fed mind, body, heart, and soul.

Children of Metresili

Children of Metresili often find success with little effort. People will often give them what they need and want. Thus, it is common for her children to be lazy and unmotivated. However, her children also are able to achieve extreme pinnacles of success, as well as become famous and rich when she is being worked with properly. Children of Metresili are prone to depression, feeling isolated, and emotional turmoil. Metresili children can also be very generous and compassionate. However, it is common for them to experience jealousy or be the victims of many jealous individuals. They are known to be extremely possessive. Many women who are children of Metresili find themselves having issues with other females, often including their own mother and sisters. Like their mother, being psychic often comes naturally, as well as the powers of empathy.

Anaisa Pye

Among the most popular Misterios is Anaisa Pye, the Metresa of bliss, joy, freedom, love, and everything that brings both bliss and joy. She is also the spirit of sensuality, feminine mysteries, abundance, and freedom. In fact, you will find that she has power and connection to almost all areas of life in one way or another. Filled with abundance, she is connected with all the good things that come with success and plenty. She is known for her overflowing generosity. Having so much, she gives it away freely, especially to her children and devotees. Anaisa is all about freedom, bliss, joy, and happiness. She is a spirit of parties and festivities, as these are the natural places where people experience fun. Here, she can also do her favorite things: dance and entertain. So it's no surprise she is connected to sensuality, sexuality, seduction, and women's powers to do all those things.

Anaisa is represented in the badji with the image of St. Anne where the saint is teaching her child, the Virgin Mary, the scriptures. Both St. Anne and the Virgin Mary represent two different puntos of Anaisa. The foundational punto of Anaisa, however—known as Anaisa Pye—is represented by the young Virgin Mary. Anaisa Pye is seen as a teenage girl who is brash, flirtatious, forward, and blunt, and loves to have fun. She can often be found laughing hysterically, dancing, and having a great time. Wherever she arrives, she will definitely become the center of the party, as people are naturally drawn in to her.

The brujo attends Anaisa by giving her beer, cigarettes, and spraying her perfume. Anaisa's color is yellow, so she will also be given yellow candles and roses. Annually she is celebrated on July 26, the feast of St. Anne.

Anaisa is married to Belie Belcan. He is the only Lwa "who can understand her and let her be herself," Mai Nancy would say. This is because she can't be tied down. Being flirtatious the way that she is, she has connections and relationships to all of the Lwases to some degree or another. As she is connected with sensuality and sexuality, Anaisa is often falsely mistaken or conflated with a prostitute or prostitution. While she does have power there and is able to help prostitutes excel professionally, she herself is not one. Like anyone who is more sensually open and free, Anaisa and her children are often attacked by society in that manner. Anaisa is not a prostitute and will tell you clearly, "I am a free woman who makes my own choices . . . not for money or need, but because I want to, choose to, and can."

She has connections to all the Misterios in one way or another.

At a ceremony, Anaisa herself explained her importance. She said:

"I am the reason why God made the world . . . to bring joy and bliss, to have that, to give that, to birth that, to bring that . . . but it took all the others to come before me, for those things to pass, in order for God to reach me and be able to make me: the last and the youngest. And that is why all the Misterios need me, and even love me although they might not like me. . . ."

Anaisa, as she said, is the youngest of all the Misterios. Because of this, she is the "most spoiled by the other Misterios" to some degree or another—she's the baby of the family after all.

Anaisa comes off as the world's best friend—meaning the best friend a person could hope to have. She keeps it blunt, straight, and real. Whether you like it or not, whether you are offended or not, she can be counted upon to be the only one to tell you the truth even when no one else will. She always has a way of lifting your spirits, no matter how deep in the dumps you find yourself. She is supportive no matter what you do and always tries to bring positivity into the matter, no matter how bleak.

She's the type of friend you would never want to lose. She doesn't play around either. She's loyal but at the same time isn't going to tolerate just anything. She won't let you get away with anything and will be quick to call you out when needed. Anaisa doesn't "have any hair on her tongue," meaning she doesn't hold back. She says exactly what needs to be said, no mincing of words. When neglected, she immediately responds and metes out the appropriate punishment. Servidores who have been lax or lazy in their responsibilities with her will be punished with money and love troubles.

Once she has mounted her horse, she will get dressed and prepare herself to help people. This can be as simple as putting on her golden fula, which she wraps on her head or as complex as a blouse, skirt, jewelry, and makeup. She will be given her perfume, which she sprays abundantly and copiously everywhere. Given cigarettes along with her favorite drink of beer and she is ready to greet those present and "work."

Anaisa Saves Eva's Relationship and Engagement

Eva was referred to me by another client. A very successful businesswoman, Eva was experiencing a different type of challenge. Her man, Daniel, had gotten cold feet, broke off their engagement, and started talking to tons of women. To make matters worse, he was hanging out with a bunch of single guys who were all about living the player's lifestyle. No matter what she said or did, he wasn't interested in fixing things with her. Daniel had gone to the extent of staying in one of these guy's houses, which was basically a bachelor pad. Eva knew that she needed to get this resolved and fast because he had shown absolutely no intention or even the slightest second thought of changing his new lifestyle. Having done the consultation for Eva, I saw that Anaisa was willing to resolve this for her.

Eva had come prepared, for the most part, and had brought some items that would link to her target. She had lucked out that day as well, because she got the last appointment. Since she was almost completely ready, she begged me to do the work at that moment. And I agreed. So I made the preparations and called upon Anaisa to come and mount to do the work. After settling and getting herself ready, Anaisa asked for a piece of parchment paper, a pencil, and three candles. Having Eva light one of the candles while calling out her lover's name, Anaisa placed it on the table. Eva was instructed to call out her lover's name repeatedly as Anaisa "signed a contract" to bring back the guy. Anaisa rapidly scribbled out some doodles on the sheet of parchment while making some secret invocations in an unknown tongue. She then took and rubbed the two remaining candles on various parts of Eva's body. Suddenly grabbing some scissors with lightning speed, she shredded the links to Eva and Daniel. She then took the shreds and tied them together as she continued chanting in an unknown language.

Anaisa then left Eva with the following instruction.

"You will put this (the shredded tied-up links) under your bed. You will put this (the contract) in your underwear for three days. On the third day, you will light these three candles and burn the paper, and he will be yours again. Then you will send (money to the horse) to make the proper servicio for me for having helped you."

Anaisa left shortly after, as did Eva. Eva carried out Anaisa's instructions to the letter, and in only four days, Daniel was back at Eva's house wanting to talk. He never left that night, and they continued to talk and work on things over the next week. By the end of the week, it was decided that he would indeed move back in and they would get back on track. He would go to gather his things and resolve whatever he needed with his friends.

Eva didn't miss a beat either. Immediately after he left, she sent over what was needed so that I could make the proper servicio to Anaisa. Eternally grateful, she additionally sent Anaisa a jewelry set that her family had received from the royal family from where they were from.

Anaisa is the mistress of perfumes and scents. There are many puntos of Anaisa that are prepared as a perfume to bring about a solution. A spiritually prepared perfume is a cologne put together of various herbs, oils, essences, and scents according to a magical recipe. By wearing it, its magic encompasses the person, which attracts or repels certain things, depending on what the perfume is prepared to do. Spiritually prepared perfumes can be made for many causes—money, love, luck, to attract good things, to keep evil away, etc. The power of scent is very well-known and recorded. Quite naturally, Anaisa knows the most powerful aphrodisiacs and love potions.

Anaisa Destroys Katie's Depression

Katie's life hadn't quite shaped out the way that she had imagined. In fact, it was quite the opposite. When Katie finally came in to see me, she was totally down in the dumps with a failed marriage, flat broke, and filled with anxiety and fear. Katie was confused and lost, and she didn't know how to take her life forward and where to go from where she had been. Since her divorce, she had just simply sat and wallowed away, sinking deeper and deeper into a depression. Life was lifeless. She felt hopeless. It was as if the sun never shone for Katie. Immediately upon laying my eyes on Katie, I could see all the negativity in her spirit and the many cracks that life had caused it. I knew just what to do.

Katie needed a special remedy from Anaisa. Katie was suffering from her broken heart and all that went along with it. We needed to heal it and bring joy back into her spirit. So I prepared two spiritual items under the punto of Anaisa Pye. This first was a spiritual bath designed to give Katie strength and healing. The second, a perfume to use daily, brought back Katie's joy, lifted her spirits, and fed her light. Once ready, I invoked the power of Anaisa into the items. From there, Katie would take the bath for twenty-one days. She would also use the perfume each day.

About a month later, Katie returned for a refill on her spiritual perfume. First, she looked ten times better. She had regained the color in her face, and she had energy and a spark to her. She remarked on the same, saying, "I feel alive again. I didn't realize how dead I had been feeling." She was excited to continue with her perfume, which she called "my lifesaver," and reported, "The first week was tough. I only felt the tiniest bit better. But suddenly in the second week, one day I woke up and everything was different—lighter and happier. From that day, things have gradually improved. I also had a few dreams: some weird ones which I want to tell you about. But the most important is I think I saw Anaisa in one of those dreams. All I remember is that it was a young woman's face, who was laughing and telling me, 'get over it' as she pointed and laughed at me. In the morning, I felt as though it was her telling me I was ridiculous for worrying. I thanked her for her help in giving me some sight, because I was totally out of it."

Anaisa Breaks the Tie on Louis

Louis was the unfortunate victim of a powerful spell known as an *amarre*, or binding spell. Louis's girlfriend had this spell cast on him when things between them were good. She was determined to keep Louis in her life forever. Louis's mother, however, didn't trust Xena, his girlfriend. She felt that Xena was a user and a gold digger. Truth be told, she was right. But due to the spell, Louis couldn't see this about Xena and refused to believe it for months. But after she abandoned Louis in jail for quite some time, Louis finally trusted his mother's impression. Even with all the harmful and hurtful things Xena had done to him, he kept going back, and he didn't know why. He had never done anything like this. He believed his mother when she said that he had been "worked upon" because he was absolutely obsessed with Xena.

He told me, "I didn't believe in these things and I certainly didn't think it would happen to me," at which point, I informed him that anyone not properly protected is vulnerable.

It's like a vaccine: it doesn't matter whether you believe in the sickness or not, if you are not protected, you can catch it, I told him.

"Well I believe now. 'Cause no matter what she does to me, I keep going back for more. I feel like I can't get her out of my head."

Anaisa is also known as the Liberator. So we called upon her to break this spell on Louis. Once she mounted, she clearly explained how it all came to be. She even told Louis the exact time when the spell had happened and described to him of various events occurring in his life at that time. As Louis put it, "I had to pick up my jaw from the floor" due to the level of accuracy and detail with which she outlined what happened to him. She touched his head, breaking the spell. Then she gave the prescription for a special cleansing I would need to do for Louis.

After she had gone, we set to prepare and do the cleansing Louis needed. Louis said, "When she touched me, I felt a shiver go up my spine. Then right as you were cleaning me, I felt something change. I don't know what it was, but I could feel it, and I felt a little like my old self." I didn't see Louis again until months later when he came to an event with his mother. "Thank you so much, Papa," he said. "I don't know what I would have done, I was going crazy." At this we all had a good chuckle. He then told me that he would be coming in later that week "to check on a girl I'm interested in; I want to make sure she's cool, because I'm not going through that again."

Anaisa Saves Steven's Job and Gets Him a New Place to Live

As an abundant queen, Anaisa has incredible power to bring in money, work, and luck at an alarming speed. In fact, Anaisa has the capacity to "turn your whole life around" in three days when she wants. That can be for the better or for the worse, depending on where you stand with her. There are many spiritual works that are done with Anaisa for financial prosperity and success.

"I met Mama Anaisa at your Anaisa ceremony. Your god-daughter Selena brought me. We worked together for many years. I was the supervisor there, but I had always and regularly had an issue with Mindy, the manager. First off, Mindy was crazy and erratic. As a spiritualist, she was a confused mess. So we never saw eye to eye. Mindy was also good friends with the owner, an old man only interested in the finances of the business.

"It was normal for Mindy and I to get into heated discussions about how various things in the shop should run. There were regular issues among the employees, which had to be managed. Mindy and a few others also seemed to love to keep the drama going. I had grown accustomed to things running this way. So when we got into an argument about how to manage an issue that some of the employees were having, I thought nothing of it. However, the next day after opening up the shop, Mindy came in and told me I was fired. I called the owner, and he told me that he backed whatever decision Mindy had made. So I was out of a job just that quick.

"That weekend is when I came to the ceremony at your house. Upon meeting me, Anaisa told me what had been going on as if she had been there watching, like a fly on the wall. She even told me, word for word, some of the things that were said between me and Mindy during the argument. Then, she got a big grin on her face, a smile from ear to ear. She said, 'If you want to be back there, I can put you back there (get you your job back), to which I started nodding yes. Then she said, 'But I'm going to want something back.'

"So we worked out an arrangement. I would bring her back certain offerings once I had my job back. She then addressed my living situation. I had been living in a boardinghouse for quite some time. It had become very stressful, however, as well as certain things of mine were going missing. She said, 'Once you bring me my things, I'll help you get out of that too and into your own space.'

"That was a Saturday. On Monday afternoon, I got a call from Mindy asking me if I would take my job back and come back to work. She asked me if I could come in right then and there. She had found out that I did much more than what she thought or than what she thought she could do. So I went in to work, and that weekend I came back to give Anaisa what I owed. She amazed me again that day, when she told me that I would get a call the next day for a new place to live. That's exactly what happened. Just a few weeks after that first party, I was in a new place."

Anaisa Saves Christine: A Business Sale

Anaisa is known to be a shrewd businesswoman. She is excellent at selling almost anything. It's part of her power of seduction: the communication that leads to a sale. When businesses are on the brink of disaster, it is very common to approach Anaisa. Because when you need speedy help, she's the one to give it to you. Along with her powers of seduction, she can attract attention to draw customers, buyers, and clients. As such, she is called upon by many salespeople or those who work on commissions and quotas.

Christine had made a very bad investment. A business that she thought would have been successful was anything but. So she resolved that the best way out of this mess would be to sell the business as soon as possible. But months had gone by and all she had had two deals fall through. She was able to attract buyers, but once they started to take a deeper look, they would cancel.

She could not waste another day, as things were quickly deteriorating. So she came in to see Anaisa. Anaisa prepared a special powder for Christine to spread all over her business. She then gave her a special oil to place on the chairs where she would have the meetings to sell the business. Anaisa agreed to get this business sold in exchange for an Hora Santa. Christine agreed and went off to follow Anaisa's instructions. Less than a month later, the business was under contract with a buyer. Christine returned to give the Hora Santa that she owed.

Anaisa's Children

Anaisa's children are extremely psychic, intuitive, and aware. They are very commonly misunderstood, as they often are said to "act crazy," which basically just means that they don't follow the rules. They say and do what they want. They have a tendency toward two different characters: on one side quiet and serene—almost shy, virginal, and pure—and on the other brash, abrasive, extroverted, fun, and loud. They are known to exude a natural sensuality or sexual force, of which they are most often aware and can and do use. As such, they are often said to be or thought of as promiscuous. They can be very dramatic for the good or for the bad and are naturally witty and sarcastic. When unelevated, their words become very cutting. When unexalted, Anaisa's children suffer from confusion, being overly dramatic, financial issues, and a lack support from others. They will often cause dramas when unelevated. When elevated, Anaisa's children bring forward joy, fun, love, and bliss. For Anaisa's children, the world's a stage and everyone's an actor. Empowered, this fills Anaisa's children with strength, joy, and happiness. Disempowered, they are disillusioned, depressed, and sad.

Division de Justicia/
Justice Division

This division is composed of all the Misterios of Justice and ruled by Belie Belcan. Sometimes this division is also called the Division Belcan. The Misterios of this division rule over creating justice and balance. In life, many of these Misterios assist in court cases, legal matters, and other such life issues. They can also be called up to serve justice or defend those who are just. Many of the Misterios of this division have lesser followings than its leader Belie.

Belie Belcan

Belie Belcan, associated with Saint Michael, is the defender of truth, justice, and everything that is right. He defends us against our enemies and defeats them for us, just as he defeated the devil. He is one of the most respected and loved Misterios in the 21 Divisions. As a Dominican patron saint, I would say that Belie has the largest following and the most devotees out of all the Misterios. He is known as a respected, honorable, benevolent king. His decisions and judgments are always wise and fair, bringing justice and balance to all.

He is seen as a short, old man who holds a machete in one hand. Even though he is old, he has some very fast reflexes. He is quick to punish his servants for their misdeeds. He has been known to destroy altars. Although he is very protective of his children, he has high expectations of them as well. Hijos of Belie Belcan often deal with issues having to do with spiritual attacks and negative spirits. By dealing with these issues, Papa Belie makes his children incredible warriors as they learn to battle by facing them themselves.

When he mounts, the horse never falls to the ground. Belie will then tie a green fula on his head and a red one across his chest. He is given his cigar, which he puffs on contentedly, and then his tafia. Some houses also give him a green and red cloak that he may don. He will be given his sword or his machete, and then he is ready to consult and work. At a Mani, he will greet the crowd with "Bonswa La Sosyete, Yo Soy Belie Belcan," meaning "Good evening to the Society (People gathered), I am Belie Belcan."

Belie is known to limp in one leg. The leg varies from horse to horse. This is due to the injury he sustained during his battle with the devil. However, he was ultimately victorious. Like everything in the 21 Divisions, the symbolism is very important. Belie, as he was fighting with the devil, ended up accidentally stabbing himself in his own leg. This signifies that when you are working with power, as symbolized by the sword, it can turn on you or harm you even with the best of your intentions and greatest care.

He is very sympathetic and friendly. He loves interacting and helping his hijos and devotos. Belie is a Misterio that gives his people strength and faith. He empowers them and makes them feel safe and secure. He is very fatherly and caring. Like one of my cousins, a bruja, says, "He enters right into your heart."

He is a gentleman with women and sometimes can be a bit shy around the ladies. He is known to be married to Anaisa Pye, and one will always find them next to each other in a Dominican badji. They assist each other in the destruction of evil wanga. Anaisa and Belie's relationship, however, is a bit different. They are not very traditional. Rather Anaisa lives her life and does her thing and Belie the same. Then they share with each other. Due to their natures, though, the relationship works.

One of his symbols and tools is scales. He is known to balance the scales when wrong has been done. As the perfect judge, he is very understanding of human frailties. Speaking in a low voice, he will let you know when you have done wrong. He will then dispense wise advice to you on how to correct your path and what you have been doing. However, balance is blind, meaning that Belie must cause balance once the deeds have been done, no matter whether he likes you or not. In this aspect, he is tied to the Baron de Cementerio, who as death is also in the place of ultimate judge.

One of his famous statements and proverbs is "Yo soy chiquito pero jodon," meaning "I am small/short but I can mess you up/I am strong-willed and pushy." Belie is a powerful warrior and can be severe. "If you don't take care, I'll kill you all" is another of his famous lines, referring to the importance of following through on your promises, obligations, and keeping clean actions. Belie is the leader of the Division of Justice. Belie is known to warn his followers when danger of improper action is afoot with "the ground is wet; be careful not to slip," meaning that it would be easy to do something wrong and end up on the wrong side of justice.

Belie Belcan's closest companion and best friend is Candelo Cedife. Belie Belcan rules over the Division of Air, while Candelo leads the Division of Fire. They assist each other in battle, fueling one another and giving each other greater power and reach. When Belie and Candelo are together, Belie becomes even more war-oriented. The winds become even more turbulent and heated, so to speak. This brings forward his battle aspect. He is commonly called upon to prepare resguardos for people. He is known to work with Candelo in order to do strong jobs. Many times Belie leaves and Candelo is the one who replaces him. They are *compadres* (best friends), and the only time they fight would be in order to claim the head of a new caballo.

Belie and Ogou Balendyo are known to have frequent battles. They sort of have a love-hate relationship. One issue between them is a jealousy over Candelo. Candelo and Ogou Balendyo used to be closer before he started spending time with Belie. Throughout the course of time, then, Ogou Balendyo has always had a bone to pick with Belie. Candelo, being caught between the two and enjoying his connection to both, stays out of their issues. However, he spends more time with Belie, as Balendyo is regularly out at war. One of the other common points of battle between the two is in terms of servidores. Like with Candelo, Ogou and Belie enjoy fighting over people's heads and claiming victory. Even with all these issues between them, they are known to bind together against common enemies.

Carla and Catalina: The War for the Head

Carla had always been called to the Misterios and over time had found various brujos to help her begin the process of unraveling her power. Through her journey, she had begun serving her

Misterios, and her life was much improved. She had a business: a corporate cleaning company that was successful and made possible by the Misterios. Her children were finally on track. Plus, her marriage, which was pretty much dead when she started, had come back to life.

She lived in Canada, so it was very difficult to find a brujo that would agree to help her unravel. But finally after many failures, she had found a bruja named Mercedes who agreed to help her. She would make a yearly trip to Canada to handle all of Carla's spiritual needs. They would be able to maintain contact by phone the rest of the year.

Carla had also introduced her sister Catalina to the Misterios over time. Seeing the breakthroughs in Carla's life, Catalina had set up her own altar and started serving the Misterios as best she could. Her life also improved. But she followed behind Carla. Since Carla had introduced her and was her eldest sister, Catalina would let Carla find the brujos and go from there.

Upon the first visit of the bruja Mercedes, she let Carla know that there's a battle over her head. The battle was between Ogou Balendyo and San Miguel. Carla was ecstatic to get this information. It was one of the issues that had prevented her from progressing further. She had studied under various brujos throughout the years, but none had been able to figure out who Carla's Misterio de Cabeza was. Now it made sense to Carla that the brujos couldn't tell, as this battle would have made it difficult to determine.

Unfortunately for Carla, however, Mercedes was not as advanced or as unraveled a bruja as she made herself out to be. Although Mercedes could see this, she thought it was as simple as Carla choosing one. So, Mercedes instructed Carla that she had to pick one, either Saint Michael or Saint James. She instructed

Carla to choose whichever one that she felt a stronger and deeper affinity for. Naturally, you cannot select your own Misterio de Cabeza; you are born with it. But Carla didn't know that. As far as she was concerned Mercedes knew what she was doing. Second, Carla, a servidora who had yet to unravel, didn't have the power to see what the right choice would even be for her.

It was a very difficult choice. Carla could see a benefit to having either of the santos. But she was currently experiencing lots of negativity in her life, so she could see the benefit of San Miguel. Still, she knew that Ogou Balendyo was also a healer and could lift those who had fallen. Not knowing what to do, Carla talked with Mercedes about her decision. Under Mercedes's guidance, Carla chose San Miguel. Mercedes told Carla that whichever spirit she did not choose would go to her sister Catalina. Mercedes then began the ritual to consecrate Carla's head to San Miguel.

That evening, Carla was woken up from her sleep. Once she was awake, Carla could hear the sound of a galloping horse, as if it was running away from her house. She made a mental note of it and fell back to sleep. Afterward Carla dreamt of a place where there was a great storm. After the storm cleared, many winds started swirling around her and forming tornadoes. The tornadoes where destroying everything in sight. At some point, a huge sword fell from the sky and plunged into the earth. The sword was standing erect in the ground. Then she was lifted up and found herself flying above the whole scene, just like an angel soaring in the clouds. The next morning when she awoke, she interpreted this dream as a confirmation of the ritual and that San Miguel was now with her. She knew that the galloping horse was Ogou Balendyo leaving.

At that same time and night, her sister Catalina was awakened by the sound of a horse galloping toward her home. Unlike

Carla, she wasn't able to fall back to sleep. She looked out her window several times to see if there was any horse. Still, she knew it was ridiculous. Who would be riding a horse in the middle of the city at this time of night? However, she was greatly unnerved and anxious. No matter how much she tried to fall back to sleep, she just couldn't. She tried desperately to do so, then just gave up. So, at four in the morning she had her first cup of coffee.

That day, the sisters came together for lunch. They talked about their experiences of the night before. To both of them, it was a confirmation of the success of Carla's initiation. Catalina, although still unnerved, congratulated her sister. She felt awful, as she had been up since early that morning and was terribly anxious, but she didn't want to ruin it for her sister.

In the following days, Carla began to feel as if something were wrong, as if something had changed, as if something had gone terribly off. She didn't totally understand it, but she knew it was connected to the choice she had made. She did have a connection to San Miguel, but there was another tie that she felt she had lost. This was the connection she had to San Santiago. At first there was peace, but now she felt anxious—empty, as if something were missing.

Her sister, on the other hand, had never really taken care of San Santiago before, nor had any affinity for him. After a few days, however, she felt calm and as if he had breathed new life into her when he arrived. She started serving Ogou Balendyo. Unlike Carla, she never went through with receiving any cere-monies, puntos, or rituals from Mercedes; however, San Santiago accepted her and adopted her to work.

Just as her dreams had predicted, Carla's life turned quickly into a state of turmoil. This was because, although Belie was there and fighting for her head, Ogou Balendyo was actually the owner and Misterio of her head. It took many years for things to shift for Carla and for her to become restablized in her life and progressing. Now, she has acclimated to Belie Belcan and is once again successful. But it was not without lots and lots of suffering due to the choice she made and the mistake. In those years she spent cleaning up the shambles of her life, Carla found herself very jealous and angry toward Catalina. Catalina's life had started improving in leaps and bounds since Ogou Balendyo came into her life. She had even started to develop powers with very little effort.

Carla felt that this was due to Catalina receiving the Ogou Balendyo that belonged to her. Carla made various attempts to convince her sister to "let him go and send him back" but failed miserably. Catalina was unwilling to do so, as she knew that many of the blessings coming through were due to Ogou Balendyo. She could recognize the amazing and miraculous influence he had in her life. This ultimately separated the sisters for quite some time until Carla finally was able to get her life back on track. At that point, she was able to let it go and move on from the situation, healing the issues with her sister. At this stage both Carla and Catalina still serve the Misterios and are living happier, more fulfilled lives due to their service.

Belie Defeats Carlos's Enemies at Work

Belie Belcan is the leader of the Celestial Militia. He uses his sword to battle evil spirits, demons, and forces. He then uses his chains to bind them. As the winner of the war against Lucifer, Belie is known to be the most powerful defense against evil. But in order to be protected by Belie, you must be in the right and you must be good with him. You must be clean-handed in your affairs and life. Otherwise justice and Belie Belcan will have no other choice but to do what is right. "The law is the law" for him, meaning no matter how much the Misterios feel for you and love you, they cannot negate the universal laws of balance.

Carlos's enemies at work had begun to really lay into him. They started gossip mills and rumor circles. They wanted him out of there. Carlos had tried everything he could think of to make peace, but that didn't work. These people didn't want peace. Rather they want Carlos to leave the job.

Carlos had been busting himself to try to get a promotion. But due to these evil speakers, he was passed up for one yet again. This had been the second time that this had occurred to him. It was becoming pointless to even try.

Belie, upon seeing him, explained all of this to Carlos. He then assured Carlos that he could assist him not only conquer and dominate his enemies, but also to receive the next promotion when it came up.

Belie left instructions for me to carry out in order for the enemies to be defeated. Then he instructed Carlos in this way:

"Starting on a Tuesday night at 9 p.m., you will light a red candle and a green candle. The red candle will be on your right side and the green candle on your left side. Between them you will place a cross. You will light the candles, and then you will smoke a cigar in my honor as you pray the 7 Swords.

"Then you will speak to me on what you need and shut off the candles. You will complete this for nine days and on the last day allow the candles to burn themselves out. Take the remains and drop them at your workplace.

"This you will do, and I will defeat your enemies for you. When I do, you will give me a grand ceremony in return.

"Once you have conquered and your enemies are under your foot, you will return and I will bring you the luck you need in order to get the promotion that you have been working for."

And so Carlos returned to give me the items needed to carry out my end of the work as he did his.

Less than a month later Carlos returned. "I need to schedule a ceremony for Belie" was the first thing he said.

The little crew that had gone up against Carlos consisted of four people. In that little bit of time, the group had been utterly destroyed. The first enemy left to a new job altogether. The second and third were transferred to other departments. The last enemy that remained, totally weakened by not having the others around, grew quiet and docile. In fact, he did everything he could to avoid Carlos.

Carlos had returned to pay Belie and to get going on getting the promotion that he had worked for years to gain.

Belie Belcan Revokes Jealousy for Paula

Belie Belcan also has connections to La Sirena, Yemaya, and the Water Division. The Indian Division is feasted on the day of Archangel St. Michael, Belie Belcan, on September 29. After destroying all evil, breaking the chains and cords by invoking Belie, the brujos then call upon the Water Misterios, particularly Yemaya, to wash away all evil. A little-known fact about Belie Belcan is that before the Middle Ages, the Archangel St. Michael was associated with water, not fire or air. San Raphael was the Angel of Air. But during this period, the two angels switched positions. When San Miguel was the angel of water, his color was blue. At times, Belie is given a blue fula due to his connection with the waters.

Belie is best-known for his power to reverse evil. He is the king of revocations, magical works that return the evil to the sender. They are usually done by filling a clear glass with some item (depending on the type of work, Misterio, and other things) and then placing a saucer over the top. This is flipped over and a candle is lit on the bottom of the glass. Revocation prayers are made for a number of days depending on the work being done. The most popular and well-known traditional revocation is known as the Revocation of San Miguel.

Paula had been dealing with a huge number of blockages for more than a decade, and deep down inside she was aware of the cause. She had felt it and known it for a long time. Her blockages and inability to progress in life were mainly due to the jealousy projected upon her by other people. This would make it so that Paula would advance only ever so slightly before being faced with a number of issues and problems that would ultimately waste any blessings. Paula was left in a state of constant fear and frustration, never knowing what to expect next. Every time something good would happen, she would understand that it was just a matter of time before something bad would occur. It was the never-ending cycle.

She constantly faced the judgments of her peers, friends, and even family members. When she did well, they were jealous of her and did their best to sabotage her. When she did badly or poorly, they acted sympathetic but couldn't actually hide their joy at her failures. Nevertheless, Paula always tried, continuing to be ambitious and courageous, pushing forward in trying to live the best life that she knew how. After visiting various brujos and psychics and not finding what she called "a fit for me," she came in to see us.

The day she showed up was the one when we called the Misterios to consult. That day it was Belie who had arrived to trabajar. Belie told her her issues and quickly the way out: he was the solution that Paula never knew she could have. He and he alone was able to protect and clear a path of all jealousy and negativity that would finally allowed Paula to be free of the chains and out of the vicious cycle. All she would have to do is agree, and he would begin.

She did. She knew in her heart it was the right choice. She could feel the love, the warmth, and the care of Belie. More than a father, this Misterio would protect and care for her.

My aplasa was given the list to give to her, and she was to return and we would call Belie to resolve for her. This she did, and that day she was consecrated as a servidora and devota of Belie Belcan. From that day forward, things began to change for her. She reported, "I immediately saw changes from people at work. They were nicer to me, friendlier, and it was authentic." And in her family, things turned around. "A healing happened . . . I don't know how or what happened, but I don't care, I know it is my San Miguel who took care of it for me." Little by little, Paula's life changed into what she never thought possible. Less than a year later, Paula reported having "a whole new life thanks to Belie" and "being alive again."

Does she still face jealousy? Sabotage? Attacks? Of course. But with Belie Belcan, none of it harms her. It doesn't reach her. It doesn't affect her or her life in any way. Not only that, but it is minimal, not like before where her life had become a source of constant issues and pain. As my grandmother would say, "If you live, you suffer, but if you live with the spirits, you have a solution."

"Now I have something I never had," she said to me.

"And what is that?" I replied, already knowing as I could see it in her.

"Peace in my life and in my mind, heart, and soul."

"*Gracias a La Misericordia, Ke Viva Belie Belcan!*" I responded.

Belie Gets a New Brujo

Belie Belcan in some lineages is considered the king of the entire 21 Divisions. As the premier archangel of God, whose name means "He who is like God," San Miguel for some brujos claims the position of leader of the 21 Divisions. You will notice that depending upon the lineage of 21 Divisions that you enter, the ultimate "Leader of the 21 Divisions" will differ. This is a secret of the lineage, and once you enter the 21 Divisions, you will come to understand this closely guarded secret and how it is used for power.

Belie Belcan can be reached directly. He is one of the most amiable and approachable of all the Misterios. As the leader of the archangels and all the angels, he is ready and willing to answer a sincere plea for help, no matter who calls. Unlike the other Misterios, who require that the gates be opened prior to being called, or who are only open to being invoked by brujos, Belie is very accessible. All that he requires is cleanliness of hands, heart, and mind—a clean faith, sincerity, and an ardent heart. Here he has a close connection with the Legba Division, serving as a sort of gatekeeper between the human plane and the angelic. Many practitioners keep the image of Belie above the door to protect and guard against evil entering the house and only allowing good to enter. A brujo will also be called upon to place Belie's punto at the door making the power of Belie serve as a guardian in that place.

Juan had come to me because he was experiencing constant loss and regression. Every time he would move forward, he would be dragged back into the same position he had been in or worse. He could never move forward or get himself out of the home he was in. Juan actually knew the root of his problem, but he didn't say a word about it.

So Juan came in for a consultation. Immediately, I saw an angry and frustrated Belie. It was clear, and I said so, "Juan, your family serves the Misterios, and you are meant to serve and work for the Misterios. . . ."

"Yes," he replied as if surprised.

"You're in a mess now because you have Belie; you're to be doing the sacred work for him. You also have Gran Tiinua with you."

There Juan's eyes lit up. As if on fire, he almost hopped out of the chair.

"You are my Padrino. It is you I've been searching for. . . . That's why I couldn't take care of the Misterios; I didn't have a lead, no one to show me the way. I've gone everywhere to find my brujo, but you are him."

I smiled as he continued.

"My family has the Misterios, but we are born with them. In my family, even with that, each person born with the Misterios must find his or her own brujo. We don't all follow the same brujo; each one has someone different. When I was a child, my grandmother told me I had the light of the Misterios. She told me that my teacher would see my spirits, but my true teacher would see Gran Tiinua. So that's what I've been looking for. . . . "

From this point on, we began the process of his unraveling. Just two months after beginning, his life had already changed.

Juan had a better job, had more money, and moved into a new place with his wife and children. A few months after that, he changed jobs again for even better money and pay. Within half a year he had begun mounting Belie at ceremonies and rituals. Due to all the great growth and success, Juan was able to prepare for bautizo initiation and became a full brujo. Soon after he had unraveled enough to begin his practice and started helping others. Belie works with him as his main Misterio to achieve all sorts of miracles for those who come to him.

Like all brujos, Juan continues to grow and unravel his power as he serves the people and the purpose.

Belie Stops Spiritual and Psychic Attacks

Belie is known to have two Centinelas that work for him: Centinelas Tribunal and Kriminal. Both of these Misterios are Petroses. They assist in attaining work, health, winning court cases, and protection. They can be dangerous and temperamental, which is why Belie keeps them in check. Centinela Tribunal assists in court cases and attaining work and health. Tribunal is a powerful Misterio that is able to turn the tables in these situations in favor of those Belie chooses. Centinela Kriminal is a very fierce Misterio, known for his love of pins, needles, spikes, and broken glass. He lives in the woods and is terrible when upset.

Nan was the unfortunate focus of an occult group that turned on her. Since their own lives were miserable, they focused on Nan because, as you know, misery loves company. They began to use their power against her and send nasty spirits to harm her and her family. Since the attacks, Nan had lost her job, her husband's job was on the line, and her children were suffering with nightmares and insomnia. It had gotten so bad that the school had grown concerned with the children and started an investigation into Nan and her husband. Nan had no recourse. She had been around to various practitioners for help and failed. Her enemies just kept at it and kept winning.

Naturally, what she needed was the help of the leader of the Celestial Militia and prince of justice, Belie Belcan. So that's the Misterio we called. Belie Belcan arrived and blessed her. Blowing copious smoke at her with his cigar, he also cleansed her with his fula by passing it over her. Then he began ringing the bell as he spoke the secret incantations over her to bless her and bring her some peace. This would help her until we had completed the work. Nan's body drooped. He also left us with the instructions we needed to turn things around.

Belie's plan was simple. She would receive his punto, and he would protect her. We were to clear all the evil spirits before the punto. Finally, we would place another punto in her home. The family would receive resguardos to protect them from the maladies. Lastly, we would send Centinela Kriminal to teach her enemies a lesson. They would stop altogether because they would be having so many issues they wouldn't even have the time to worry about Nan.

So we began the work we could do at that time for Nan and scheduled the rest. We sent the Centinela that night to begin his work on the group as well.

When Nan returned just a few days later, she reported that since that day she was able to sleep and get some rest. But also her children, whom we had yet to treat, were calmer and getting more sleep. She dreamt on Friday night that an angel came to visit her, but she couldn't remember the fine details. She recognized that this was San Miguel and she thanked him the next morning. "At that time my faith and hope grew more firm. It was already firmer when I left, but that dream changed something for me," she said. So we proceeded with the rest of the treatments that she needed. We went over to her home and placed the punto.

In the end, the leader of the group working against her had a terrible car accident. Naturally this put the group out of business. But it seemed Centinela Kriminal wasn't finished. The other main leaders all came to accidents and calamities of varying degrees. Several lost their jobs; one eventually lost their home. It was an absolute mess for them. Two ended up with grave illnesses. One fortunately was able to recover; the other was not.

Most importantly, Nan's house and home were filled with peace again. The case against her and her husband was dropped. The children were able to sleep. She was able to sleep too. The constant battle and fighting in her life subsided and disappeared. She was able to focus again on her goals and happiness. All of this occurred in less than three weeks. Nan had returned to give her offerings to Belie and to get his help in getting her career on track again.

To serve Belie, you should give him a glass of rum and a cigar. An image of St. Michael should be there. His colors are red and green, and a candle of the appropriate color should be given to him. Belie's favorite rum is Brugal, the national rum of the Dominican Republic. A sword is also frequently a tool that is placed on his altar.

Belie's favorite food is goat meat. Not all lineages practice animal sacrifice within the 21 Divisions, but in the lineages that do, a black goat signifying Lucifer may be sacrificed to Belie Belcan. This signifies Belie's ultimate conquering of the devil, the fight between good and evil, in which good wins. The meat is then properly cooked and served to Belie. Only a properly trained priest has the right and permission to perform animal sacrifices.

In lineages that do not sacrifice, the meat will be purchased, cooked properly, and then given to Belie Belcan.

Children of Belie Belcan

Hijos of Belie are faithful and loyal, and make friends and connections easily. They can also be extremely judgmental, however, and destructive when upset. They are often just when clear, and they stand for justice and what they believe is right. This is what most greatly upsets them: when they feel that what they think is right has been violated. They are kind and can be very understanding when they are good with Belie. They are usually hard workers and honest.

Division de Agua Dulce/ Sweet Water Division

The Division of the Indians forms the third leg of the triad that forms the 21 Divisions. It's known as the Sweet Water Division because it's connected to all sources of freshwater. The strongest link is to the river, but includes lakes, lagoons, ponds, and freshwater streams and springs. Naturally, the natives set up their villages close to these sources of water. This division is well known in the Dominican Republic, but the Indian Division is almost nonexistent in Haitian Vodou.

Los Indios, or the Indians, are made of the spirits of the Taino and Arawak nations that originally inhabited Hispaniola and the Caribbean Islands. Unfortunately, little remains historically about the Taino culture. Most of the Tainos, who were estimated to have numbered between a quarter to half a million people, were completely wiped out by Christopher Columbus and European invaders due to infectious diseases carried to their shores and the atrocities committed against them. Less than thirty years after the arrival of Columbus, only 10 percent of the original population remained.

The Taino were gentle, friendly, and peaceful people. They were also considered to be naive and known for their honesty and generosity. *Taino* means brother or sister. They were a highly organized culture that extended all throughout the Caribbean Islands. In fact, there are known to be a few different "types" of Tainos. Taino chiefdoms were ruled by a leader known as a *cacique*. In Dominican Voodoo, a number of famous caciques were elevated and became Misterios. Two of the most historically as well as spiritually famous are Anacaona and Caonabo. She was a Taino princess and he a warrior prince. Together, they lead this division.

Caonabo was a chief of the Manguana tribe, which ruled over a section of the island now part of the Dominican Republic. Caonabo led a number of rebellions against the Spanish and was eventually captured and died by their hands. Enriquillo is another very famous warrior of this division. Another historical figure that was elevated to Misterio, Enriquillo was a military general for his people.

Anacaona is highly revered in the 21 Divisions and has great importance as the queen and female leader of the Agua Dulce Division. She is connected to Anaisa. Some lineages see her as one of Anaisa's *vueltas*. Her sacred color is orange, as well as red. She is a water Metresa and loves perfume, which she requires to be sprinkled around her generously. She receives her servicio with beer, a red candle, an oil lamp, and her fresh fruit. Brujos give her cigars and tobacco.

Anacaona was also a real, living person, who was a warrior princess and then became chief among her people. She ruled a section of the island now located in Haiti. She had a great love for her people, whom she treated like her children and supported to the very end, although she was so young. She was a poet and singer. Married to Caonabo, she was a woman of great power, known for her strength and patriotic spirit. At only twenty-nine, she was eventually hung when captured, being accused of conspiracy by the Spanish.

Tin Djo Alagwe is among the most famous and popular Misterios of this division. He is represented by the image of Saint Raphael the archangel. His colors are pale blue and pink, and he is given offerings of fish, fresh fruits, and water. When he mounts a horse, he needs fresh water to be sprinkled over him constantly and breathes deeply and vigorously. Without this regular water put on him until he is drenched, he can heat quickly and become upset. Once he is completely soaked, he can consult and perform healings. He is given a nice, thick, lit cigar, and he begins his work. He also loves beer. Tin Djo doesn't speak much or often, but he does have the capacity to do so.

Rey del Agua is the king of water. He can be found at the mouth, or beginning, of a river. He walks with a staff, and if you possess spiritual vision, you can see him at times dredging through the water.

La India de la Agua Azul, or the Indian of the Blue Waters, was a well-known Indian priestess and is sometimes represented by the image of the Stella Maris or Our Lady Star of the Sea. This image is also used to represent Yemaya, another Misterio. She makes powerful cleansings and healings. Although the body of water in the image was originally the sea, when used to represent La India, it is evocative of blue, freshwater ponds and pools. It's this water that she uses to clear and cleanse. Her power is like a refreshing waterfall and provides healing to the heart and emotions.

Indio de la Paz is the Indian of Peace who possesses the power to make peace in any situation. When he mounts, he sits cross-legged on the floor and is tied with green and white fulas. He is a dry Indian of the forest; however, he works with water. With rum and cigars, he is attended. Some brujos keep a large head-dress made of many feathers as often seen with Indian chiefs. He arrives singing a healing song that shifts the forces of the environment immediately. He has great wisdom and does sit and consult.

Carmelina Dan Soley is a powerful Metresa who is connected to the sun. She brings powerful penetrating healing rays when invoked properly. She favors bright yellows and gold. She brings prosperity, abundance, healing, and energy to her devotees. Her favorite fruits are oranges, pineapples, and grapefruit. She enjoys beer and cigarettes. Citrus perfumes are sprayed in abundance for her.

Indio Bravo is the aggressive young warrior, full of fire. He is always angry and ready for battle; his eyes are crossed when he first mounts his horse. He will carry a double-headed axe that he uses in battle. He also has his bows and arrows for hunting. Once mounted, he is tied with green and red, given dark rum and cigars, and then he is ready to work. He is a great protector, and the brujos know how to call him to track down enemies and retaliate against them. There is a powerful trabajo in which a brujo can have him track down your enemy like a rabid dog. From there, I'm sure you can imagine what happens.

In general, the Indios are not the talking types. In possession, many of them prefer to use sign language and gesturing in order to communicate. Some of them do speak, just not often. They also communicate telepathically with brujos who have that capacity.

Although the Indians are associated with water, some of them are known not to like it. So there are two types of Indians: Those that are of the water are *mojao* or wet. The others are known as *seco* or dry. Those that are Indios de Agua or mojao usually require some type of water when mounting the horse. For example, Tin

Djo is an Indio de Agua. Those that are dry do not like water poured on them.

Known for its healing power, the Sweet Water Division also brings success, clarity, and abundance. However, this group is so large and encompasses all the spirits of the natives so that you can find a Misterio of every type here—warriors, soldiers, shamans, etc. This division forms a total group in and of itself.

Aside from the 21 Divisions, there's also an entire tradition and spiritual sect that deals intensely and solely with this one. Here many of the remaining practices of the Tainos were kept and remain a part of the healing work done. This is the same as the way that Petro has Gaga as a separate yet connected tradition, which we will come to soon.

This division doesn't "go with" many of the others. Particularly, the Agua Dulce Division must be kept away from the Petroses and the Black Division. We say that they do not get along, but that just means that the forces don't go together, Petros being pure fire and the Indians water. Also, the Petroses represent the Creole people, those of mixed blood, who would later betray the remaining Indians. With that being said, however, they are known to have good relations and connections with San Miguel and the Soley Division. The Soley Division is comprised of the Misterios of the sun, moon, and celestial bodies. They rule over illumination, wisdom, and knowledge. They are feasted along with Belie Belcan on September 29, as are the other archangels. Both the Agua Dulce and San Miguel work and bring about the blessings of balance. The Indians are known for having a great sense of justice, understanding, and fairness. Their wisdom is highly regarded, as they are known to "waste no words." Likewise, the Taino religion originally was primarily focused on the sun and moon, which makes the connection to the Soleys clear.

As can be expected, this division is suspicious of those who do not belong to their group. Many of them are represented by using images of stereotypical "Indians" and have no Catholic correspondence. Catholic rituals are not used in working directly with the Indians. In fact, many of them find it offensive. However, a few of them are still represented by saints. Another interesting image that's used is the three *potencias* or powers, which comes from Venezuela. They consist of Maria Lionza, el Negro Felipe, and Guacaipuro, which are major spirits within the traditions of that country. Here it represents the Division of Sweet Water.

The punto of Agua Dulce is one of the important ones for brujos to receive. It is also one of the major medicines he can confer to another. During a bautizo, the initiate is taken to a river to receive the punto of this division. The punto bestows clarity; it clarifies spiritual abilities, prosperity, and healing. We also work with this division for all the aforementioned as well as spiritual cleansings.

In the brujo's badji, a separate section is constructed for the Indians. In its simplest form, it will consist of a clay jar of water and other ingredients. Other more elaborate forms may have a small pond or pool filled with water. Images of the Indians may or may not surround the space or the pot, known as a *tinaja*. This is where the brujo will attend and work with them for prosperity, flow, and healings. Some brujos keep a huge pond or outdoor pool filled with healing waters for the Indians. The Indians will be given servicios of water, fresh fruits, herbs, coconuts, and tobacco. Stones are also connected with the Indians and offered to them. Thus, some altars have many stones.

It's also common for rituals to the Indians, healings, servicios, puntos, and so on to be held in or around a natural source of water. Brujos will go into woods, caves, mountains, rivers, and so on in order to serve and work with different Indians. There are certain sacred locations throughout the island where the Indians practiced their own rituals that are considered especially powerful. Other locations have ruling Indian Misterios that can only be worked with there. In the Dominican Republic, it's not at all uncommon for a brujo-to-be to get "taken away and instructed by the Indians" and taught healing techniques and rituals.

Due to the history of the Taino people, they are said to like and connect with those who have Taino blood. However, that's true on only one level. On another level, the powers and forces of God for which they act are a part of and affect all people.

Toni, a brujo of Santiago, serves an Indian who "lives at the bottom of the river." Once every few years, he does a servicio at the river for his main spirit. He told me, "When that Indian wants his service (in the river), I will find a white feather near the front door. Soon after that I will dream with him, and he will tell me when he wants the feast. Then I'll prepare all the foods and items and go with my people down to the river. At the riverside, I'll lay out my offerings and get in the water so that I can start calling him."

When it comes to having an Indian Misterio, it is usually a longer process of discovery. Many times, various Misterios from the division will come to investigate and check the person out. They will be doing the due diligence before showing themselves. Eventually the Misterio that belongs to the person will come to the forefront. Although the person will develop a connection with that Misterio, who will begin to teach, guide, and work with him, he will also need to care for the group as a whole. When it comes to this division and working with them, the brujo must take proper care of the entire tribe.

Children of the Sweet Water Division

Children of the Sweet Water Division are less common than for the other Misterios. They have a range of ways of being, just like the water. However, they tend toward being suspicious of others. They are shy and hold back in communication, even when things are elevated and good. They are naturally inclined toward being loyal and fair, good-natured and kind. They also have a bit of a jovial way about them even when things are rough. Enjoying the simple things, many are still hard workers. When unelevated, they lose motivation and force to complete tasks. They stagnate, and this can turn into laziness. The natural cautiousness becomes paranoia. Going into fits of rage, sudden bursts of anger, or becoming despondent will come forward. When someone is a child of one of the Indians, we say he belongs to the division as a whole.

Division Petro/Petro Division

The Misterios Petroses, or Petro Mysteries, are spirits of war and strength. Known for their aggression and wildness, they are said to live in the wilderness. Unlike the White Division, the Petroses are associated with fire and called "bitter." They are less refined, and many of them have connections to the various raw forces in nature.

This division actually contains a quarter of the Misterios. Most of the Petroses don't talk. However, some of them have *puntos de trabajar*, or working points, in which they speak. For the most part, they communicate through symbolism, gesturing, and psychic messages.

Like many things in the 21 Divisions, the Division Petro is quite controversial, and there are many different stances, views, and beliefs about them. To some they are demons—period. For many others, they are the aggressive, violent, and at times malicious Misterios. Yet others hold them to simply be the Misterios that rule over wild and savage forces.

In the 21 Divisions, the Petroses are often given blood and animal sacrifices, at least by those who perform such practices.

As previously stated, animal sacrifice is another area of conflicting opinion. Because of the sacrifices, some practitioners do not consider the Petro Mysteries to be good.

To complicate matters further, the Petroses are known to have a looser morality. They commonly aid and assist malevolent sorcerers. They are often willing to harm someone for a price.

For all of these reasons, the Petro Division is not a major focus among the majority of servidores, with some exceptions. There are a few Petroses that are considered friendlier and more approachable by people. However, for the most part, only brujos work with Petroses directly, while all others approach through priests.

Most brujos work with these Misterios for protection, spiritual battles, and very difficult cases. Some brujos have a Petro they work with magically for their clients. Many of the chief Misterios have Petroses among their courts and assistants. You'll also want to remember that any Misterio can also become *enpetrosao* meaning "aggressive when offended." Another thing to note is that there are a number of Misterios who are in other divisions who are also Petro, such as Ogou Badagris, who although an Ogou and belonging to the Division de Ogounes, is known to be Petro. He is served according to the Petro rites and rituals.

The Petroses are also closely connected with the Black Division. You'll see that many of the Petroses also have puntos in the Division of the Cemetery. It is very common to see an altar where the Petroses and the Black Division are sharing the space.

The Petroses are Misterios that emerged as a result of slavery. Revolutionary, wild, and warrior-oriented, they arose from the need for the enslaved to have protection and freedom. Petro rituals were founded by a slave known as Don Pedro, who created a community based on the service of the Petro spirits who discovered him.

Don Pedro was special. Filled with the fire and passion of the spirits, he was tired of the injustice, the torment, and the torture of his people and slavery. Under the guidance of these Petro spirits, Don Pedro began a new type of ritual to focus the energy of fire and war.

He brought his people back to life, reminding them of their power and magic. His rituals centered around a fire. Whips and chains were being snapped. The drum rhythms sped up and the dances grew frenzied with passion. The people rallied around him and joined. Little by little, he created his community, slowly taking over a whole town.

At that point, he had grown too powerful, and the Dominican government had to take action. So they proceeded to go in and destroy the commune of Don Pedro and capture him. Their plan was to execute and make an example of him.

But Don Pedro and the Misterios were a step ahead. Don Pedro managed to escape to Haiti. There not only did his rituals and Misterios continue to blossom, but his mission continued and succeeded in setting fire to the Haitian Revolution—the only successful slave revolt in history.

In some regions, the Petroses are celebrated by a special sect known as Gaga. Gaga is a whole and unique tradition, connected with the Misterios. We will not cover it fully here, but briefly, Gaga is practiced in groups of the same name. A huge part of the ritual centers around music, dance, and song. Gaga has its own distinctive type of music and dances. Gaga bands go out traveling and making their music and dance. Gaga is also a celebration of fertility, and their magic increases protection and fertility.

In my experience, the further away you get from the border of Haiti, the less you find the Petroses being worked with. The closer you are to the border, the more Haitian influences you see in the practices. This brings about a greater emphasis and acceptance of the Petroses and their power.

The Petroses prefer to be served outdoors, in nature. Although brujos keep Petroses on the altar, often we must make a trip into nature to do the work with them. They do not care to be indoors, and so they will visit but they won't stay. They want the open air, the woods, and the mountains. They love their freedom and don't like to feel tied down.

Not all of the Petroses took on the images of Catholic saints. Some of them aren't associated with any Catholic counterpart. Due to the religious history of the Dominican Republic, this led to many of them not being served or worked with. Over time, their servicios, nature, and knowledge have faded away with the passing of the elders. Although some people still know the names of the various Petro Misterios or a bit of knowledge about them, many do not have a full grasp of these spirits. Therefore, they continue to fade further away.

Many of the Petroses are known to be very jealous over their servidores—often to the point that they won't allow a servidor to work with other Misterios. Or they will limit which other Misterios the person can work with. Likewise, certain other Misterios will not work closely with someone who works with certain Petroses. Another point to keep in mind is that aside from the 21 Divisions, there are also a few other sects of work that would exclude one from working with certain Misterios.

Gran Torolisa

Gran Torolisa is the king and chief of the Division of Petroses. He is envisioned as a three-horned bull. When he mounts, he often arrives grunting and charging at people and walls. Gran

Torolisa leads the family Toro (bulls). The Catholic image used to represent him is called the Jesus of Good Hope or *Jesus de la Buena Esperanza*. Like most all of the Misterios, Gran Torolisa is a healer. He brings forth raw fiery energy, the force of vitality. With this power, he carries the strength to bust through obstacles and obstructions. Just as a charging bull breaks through walls, so does Gran Torolisa knock down whatever stops or obstructs his servidores. Like many of the Petroses, he is very strict and exacting in his ritual demands. He doesn't hold back, and he's quick to punish an error—whether it was intentional or not.

He also fights against one's enemies and injustice. Gran Torolisa hates injustice and brings about swift justice. He is often invoked by brujos for clients in court cases or having problems with the law. Torolisa is a defender of the poor and downtrodden. He can be called upon by those facing the hardest difficulties. However, if the trouble is debt, he can also be invoked to help find and bring about a solution.

As the leader of the division, he is actually one of the most approachable and "safe"—if you could use that word with any Misterio. I mean, none of the Misterios are necessarily safe. Any of them can and will punish offenses. All of them have the capacity to heal or kill. It's a grave error to respect or fear some Misterios over others. Although some may be more patient and understanding, these sympathies do run out no matter whom we are talking about. In my experience and lifetime, I've seen harsher punishments and even more death doled out by the Misterios of the White Division than I've seen done by the Petroses and Black Division. This is likely for two reasons. First, people work with the White Division more commonly and more often. So there are more chances to mess up. Second, many people mistakenly do not fear the White Division like they do the Black Division and the Petroses. So when a warning is given by the Black Division and the Petroses, people are quick to take heed and correct themselves. Unfortunately, they don't apply this same knowledge to the White Division, and they really should. As my Madrina Nancy would say, "La misma medicina, veneno." (The same thing which is your medicine can also poison you.)

That is why there is a proper path, teachers, and the tradition. Moving and being a person of honor and respect are the first right move.

At one ceremony I attended, the entire family of Toros seemed to come down at the same time. There were eight or nine different Caballos de Misterios all possessed by the various Toros, and they were in full swing. All of them were charging all over the room. Two of them were charging at each other. The Bokos and Mambos in attendance had to step and send a few of them away in order to ensure the safety of the congregation. Some of the caballos were *lobo* (wild), and their possessions were dangerously violent. They were grunting, huffing, scratching at the ground with their feet just like angry bulls in a pen. After quite some time, one of the Lwa Toro was calmed enough for him to begin to impart messages. He gestured and grunted, charged and moved in various patterns. The brujos present interpreted his messages to those he was trying to communicate with.

I remember a few of his messages and treatments that evening. One person he claimed as his child. He also told his newly claimed child that he was upset with him and that was the reason this child was dealing with legal issues. He was advised to come to see the brujo after the ceremony. Another individual was reprimanded for not fulfilling a promise that was due. Gran Torolisa explained that San Miguel would be serving justice for this offense if it wasn't corrected soon. Then there was a frail, older woman who wobbled up to the intense bull. He briskly swooped over and picked her up. He swung her around like an empty sack. Then he asked for oil and rum and began rubbing her limbs with one hand as he traced designs with the fingers of the other. She walked more firmly immediately when she stepped away from him when he was done.

Gran Bwa

Gran Bwa is the Misterio of the woods. This is the home of all the Petroses and, in fact, the original home of all the Misterios. *Gran Bwa* literally means Big Wood, and as can be expected, he embodies virility, strength, and stability. His color is green like the leaves on all the trees.

When he mounts, Gran Bwa often leaps up and down. If indoors, the congregation must assure the horse doesn't bang his head on the ceiling. Outdoors, he is also known to climb trees extremely quickly. One second, he's on the ground; the next he's up in a tree. As a spirit with tons of active energy, Gran Bwa teaches about the process of growth.

In one of his older puntos, he comes forth as a strong and stable ancient tree. Here he will often bestow the wisdom of the trees by teaching the congregation. He possesses all the knowledge of the woods, the trees, and the plants. The trees have been witnesses to life since the beginning of time.

Quite naturally, he's a master herbalist and knows all the magic contained in plants. Whenever a servidor or brujo enters the woods, they acknowledge Gran Bwa as they are entering his territory. Like many Misterios, this name is not his real name. His real name, like many others, is a highly guarded secret. It has the power to destroy or create illness with frightening speed. Gran Bwa is also known as a sorcerer and is actually a part of a sorcerous fraternity. This fraternity of Sorcerer Misterios and how to work with them make up another arcane and powerfully rare secret of the highest order.

Zili Danto

Zili Danto is a Metresa of protection, motherhood, and war. She is a fierce warrior queen. She is a patroness of mothers, lesbians, and single women. She's best known for always having her double-edged dagger in hand. Zili Danto is a spirit who is a disciplinarian. She can be found among the Petroses or in the Black Division. She is among the Petroses who actually enjoy being served inside the home. She takes care of the children, the household finances, as well as being a businesswoman.

Known for her capacity to protect and reverse and remove witchcraft, Zili Danto is invoked by brujos to do exactly these things. She is also an expert market woman, who maintains herself and her children through her sale of black pigs, which she also raises, and sometimes she can be found selling fried pork. For this reason, it is a black pig that is her favorite sacrifice, and she absolutely loves eating fried pork.

It wasn't until the mid to late '90s that Zili Danto's service and following began to really arise among Dominican brujos. Before that, although she appeared on the altar among the Black Division, her role was comparatively minor. Often referred to as *La Metresa Haitiana*, or the Haitian Metresa, she was a major focus of Haitian brujos and widely perceived as more connected to them. In the same way, many Haitian brujos consider Santa Marta (Lubana) as a Dominican Misterio to be worked with by

Dominicans. In fact, among some of the older brujos I know, this is still the way they see it.

St. John the Baptist/Jean Petro

St. John the Baptist encompasses many Misterios. Depending on lineage and the brujo, you may find him associated with a variety of different spirits. In my lineage, it is common to associate one image with many different Misterios. There are secrets to working this way that allow you to delve deeply into the Secret Keys of the Mysteries. St. John the Baptist holds many secrets as to the true nature of things and is the special patron of baptism.

He is approached by brujos and servidores for all types of things. He is invoked for protection, clearing and good luck, to find a lover or return a lover, for fertility of land, man, or beast. He is also a profound mystical teacher and healer. Really there is no limit to what can be asked of St. John the Baptist.

In his punto of Jean Petro, he is the father of Ti Jean Petro. He is a serious Lwa, who provide sage advice. He is given a dagger, and his sacred colors are green and yellow. He loves to puff on a good cigar while drinking his tafia. Jean Petro was the main Lwa of Don Pedro, the future Misterio. It was Jean Petro who gave the *reglas,* or rules and traditions, of the Petro rituals. The dagger, which serves as his symbol, is often found among all Petro motifs. It was Jean Petro who first unlocked the secrets of Petro sacrifice and its magic.

Jean Petro is envisioned as a wise, muscular, vibrant, and charismatic man approximately forty to fifty years old. He lives in the woods, where he has a band of Centinelas and Lwases that work with him and follow him. Like many of the other Petroses, he doesn't like to be "tied down." He prefers life as a nomad in the forest.

He is celebrated on June 24, St. John's Eve, with various festivities, again depending on the lineage. In my lineage we do a special cleansing and then a special bonfire. In some areas of the Dominican Republic, there are sacred locations where miracles occur at this time. At some sites, sacred holes in the ground miraculously fill with healing water. In others, sacred trees or stones bleed, sweat, or otherwise behave miraculously. Many receive beautiful blessings from St. John the Baptist during these celebrations, and he gains many new followers each year.

Ti Jean

Ti Jean is a very powerful Petro Misterio and much beloved by his devotees. He is represented by the famous image of John the Baptist as a child holding a lamb. We call him *San Juan de La Conquista,* or St John the Conqueror. Thus, he is known for his powers of overcoming any obstacle, defeating enemies, and overpowering the strong. He has the capacity to make people "gentle as lambs" and is called upon to provide all sorts of favors.

Not only does he belong to the Petroses but also to the Division Marassa. From my teachers and their teachings, I've learned that he has two main ways he likes to show himself, but he actually has the power to shapeshift in order to conquer and resolve. In one form he shows up like a young, innocent-looking boy. In another he is like a dwarf, sometimes with a stumpy leg. Ti Jean is known to have a limp, be missing a leg, be pigeon-toed, or even have no feet at all. But do not be fooled: he is no child, and leg or no leg, he is incredibly capable of doing whatever he needs to do—including climbing trees!

His favorite colors are purple and yellow. He loves fire and candy. Although a Petro, he also is known to work in the Black Division and in that punto takes on some of Gede's energy. He is a very generous Lwa but also severe. What he demands, he expects without fail, delays, or hesitation, for he's quick to punish.

Jan Fewo

When we see the image of St. Mark of the Lion, brujos see Jan Fewo. Jan Fewo has the power to call down other Misterios. With his touch and certain words, he is able when in possession of a horse to cause other horses in the room to become mounted. He also has the power to calm and pacify Misterios, as well as the heads of Caballos Lobos. He is a spirit of domination, and he sometimes works with Santa Marta and her sisters.

Gran Zero

Gran Zero can be seen working in the Petro as well as the Black Division. As *San Deshacedor* (Saint Undoer), he has the power to undo anything positive or negative. His possessions are violent, but rarely seen. In his Petro punto, he manifests as an elder sorcerer who is very demanding and loves to yell orders. As I said he rarely mounts, so he is more commonly interacted with in the spiritual form.

He knows the magic of creating "ground zero"—an empty space that provides clarity for new creations to become manifest. He is best-known for undoing black magic, hexes, and amarres or magical ties. He has the capacity to undo spells made by cord or knot magic. He is associated with St. Mary Undoer of Knots, and they can be invoked by brujos in secret rituals to undo even the most powerful magical ties.

Lwa Kriminal

The Lwa Kriminal is the head of his own family of Lwa, all of which are Petro. Among them are Jean Kriminal, Ogou Kriminal, and Ezili Kriminal. The Misterios Kriminal are even hotter and more aggressive than most of the other Petroses. If the Petroses are a bonfire, the Kriminales are a burning building. They love sharp objects, like pins, daggers, and needles.

Kriminal, the head and father of the family, is the most even-tempered of the crew. His age and wisdom help to keep his things in order. Even though he's the head of the group, the most common Kriminal to be served is Jean Kriminal. This is because he more frequently mounts those who serve him. Many of the other Kriminales mount with way less frequency.

The Division Kriminal as you may have assumed is often thought of as being made up of spirits of criminals. This is a mistake, however. Rather this division is able to approach situations from different angles that are not visible to the normal person. They are ferocious and will use any means necessary to complete a task. They are unbound and wild, so they are not concerned with social standards of justice or war.

Other Misterios

In this book, I've only been able to cover but a small number of the Misterios. They are the most popular ones with the biggest followings and form much of the foundation of the 21 Divisions. But as I stated early on, there are many, many Misterios: more than I will be able to list here. Here are some of the other common Misterios we have not been able to touch on:

Prin Gede

Luis Gede

Gede Kafou

Gede Vi

Gedecito

Ti Mazaka

Baron La Kwa

Baron Samedi

Baron Kriminel

La Gunguna

Guatapie Afinado

Marta Pye

Mama Mambo

General Danbala

Legba Manose

Rosita Legba

Zaka DiPye

La Sirena

Yemaya de Norte

Yemaya de Sud

Cachita Tumbo

Ezili Alaila

Mama Buyita

Amalia Belcan

Demanye Belcan

Gran Soley

Ti Soley

Marasa or Marassa

Loko

Papa Sobo

Agwe Tawoyo

Bosou

Bosou Twa Kon

Gran Ibo

Metresa Kanga

Simbi Andezon

Mama Chimbi

Mama Chamba

Jan Zonbi

Similo Pye

Zabalo or Sabalo

Getting Started on the Path

This chapter is intended to be a guide for you in getting started in the 21 Divisions. I've written it out for those looking toward the spiritual path and feeling the call of the Misterios. Like all things in the 21 Divisions, the first step is to schedule a consultation with the Misterios via a brujo. This is the best and proper way to begin walking the path. There is no substitute for an apprenticeship with a great brujo. The truth is that you can only advance so far without one. There is no way around that. This is not a completely solitary spiritual path.

Many try to go about it on their own, especially in the United States, where the culture of "anyone can do anything" is so strong. The truth is anyone *cannot* do anything. No matter how much a man may desire to become pregnant naturally, if he is a male, he won't. So that's a falsity. Another cultural structure that doesn't translate into Dominican Voodoo is the concept of one's "right to knowledge or information." This is markedly different from American and European culture in which it's widely believed that everyone has the right to be privy to all spiritual knowledge or information. In fact, in the 21 Divisions, a person doesn't have any such rights. Rather it's through the grace of God and permission of the Misterios that sacred knowledge is dispensed and dispersed.

One must consider that if one is actually interacting with the actual Misterios, one is dealing with spirits of the highest order and closest to God—Divine beings. Many mistakenly believe they are in contact with Misterios, when in reality they are dealing with lesser entities. They find themselves shocked when they finally do interact with the true Misterios. The Misterios demand respect by the mere fact that they are sent down to work with us by the grace and mercy of God. In order to approach the Misterios one must be pure of intention, mind, body, and spirit.

Starting on your own until you are pointed in the right direction can be okay to a certain degree. To begin with, pray to God and then to your guardian angel and Papa Legba to help you find your way to your brujo—to bring the two of you into contact. Speak your intentions and tell them you need and want their help.

First, you should know that some Misterios are more approachable than others. Not all of them are as friendly as they may seem. Most Misterios are very strict about how they should be approached and worked with. Other Misterios have forces that, unless you understand and are ready for them, you don't want to unleash or unlock. The Misterios that are safest for you to approach are generally the leaders of the major divisions. Notably, Papa Legba, one of the Black Division Misterios (Baron de Cementerio, Papa Gede, Santa Marta), Belie Belcan, and Candelo are very common Misterios that bring people onto the spiritual path. They are not the only ones, however. Any Misterio can call a person into service. My own journey started with Sirena, a mystical mermaid. Also, the Misterio who starts you on your path may or may not be a major Misterio in your life later on, though most often he or she is.

There are many steps in development and acquisition of fuerza or spiritual power. It's important not to rush and to understand that when it comes to attaining power, rarely are things easy and convenient. Remember to attain greatness, great sacrifices are made, and this is well-known among Dominican brujos. Second, if you live outside of the Dominican Republic or where there are large Dominican communities, it's likely that you're going to have to travel. Third, it is one thing to attain power, it is another to be able to manipulate it, yet another to control it and do so well, and then still another in mastering it. The acquisition of power is a marathon, not a sprint. It is a journey. I also suggest rereading the chapter on the brujo.

Generally speaking, if it's confirmed in consultation that you are meant to be a servidor or devoto de Misterios, the next step will be to receive either puntos or a refresco de cabeza. You will also need to undergo various cleansings and purifications. You'll undergo training, which is usually done via consultations with your teacher. In this way, your brujo will guide you and teach you how to serve and work with your Misterios.

Once ready, you'll be instructed to set up an altar. This will be "mounted" properly by your godparent in a special ritual. Generally, if you're just meant to be a devoto or servidor, once this has been completed your foundation is set. From then on, you'll continue to check in every so often via consultations with your Padrino. You'll also fulfill certain yearly spiritual responsibilities to your Misterios via your brujo or Papa.

Now, if through the first consultation or any of the ones that came after that, you are called to be a Caballo de Misterio or brujo, then you're process of growing the power continues. As you develop, you'll receive other puntos or ceremonies as indicated by the Misterios. You'll continue to undergo the various initiations and trainings that you need until you reach where the Misterios intend. As your power grows, so does your responsibility.

Establishing an Altar

A person who is not a brujo or bruja cannot actually have a badji or santuario, although they may have a whole room set aside for spiritual work. A badji or santuario requires a certain preparation that can only be accomplished by a proper brujo. However, all servidores can have an altar. It is even better if that altar is "spiritually mounted" by a brujo. However, if that's not possible for whatever reason, a servidor can still have an altar to the Misterios. It's very important that you set it up according to proper guidance from a teacher. In that way the altar is properly made to correspond to you spiritually.

In the old days and ways, an uninitiated servant or servidor could keep a small household altar on the floor only. Only initiates and initiated servidores would be allowed to use tables. An initiated servidor would be allowed to keep the altar on a low, short table. If a person was a brujo or on that path of development, the size would grow. Likewise, offerings and the types of offerings that can be made at the various altars differed. These days, however, servidores, initiated and not, keep altars on a low coffee table, shelves, and cabinets.

How the altar is set up and the placement of the objects on the altar are important and hold significance. This is why it is important to have proper guidance. The altar is a portal for the spiritual world and its forces. Certain Misterios don't care to be near each other on the altar, certain ones only care for certain areas, and so on and so forth.

In the 21 Divisions there is an entire system of making offerings and when such offerings should be given, to which Misterios, and so on, depending on what is needed for the person on whose behalf the brujo is offering. Making correct offerings brings balance, healing, success, happiness, and stability. Likewise making incorrect offerings causes confusion, imbalances, and more issues. Offerings constitute a whole spiritual science and school of knowledge. As a result, it's most common for most people to simply have the brujo make the larger offerings on their behalf. Devotos and servidores have certain offerings they can make that are considered generic and therefore safe. Depending on where the servidor is meant to unravel, he or she will also be instructed in other servicios.

Building a Household Noninitiate Altar

You will need a large cross to go in the center. You'll also need images or statues of the Misterios that will be served. If you want to be the most traditional, this altar should be on the floor. If not, these days it has become acceptable to use a low table, such as a coffee table. A large glass of water should also be in the center of the table. A few candles, an incense burner, and a few vases for flowers complete what you need. When you are just beginning, less is more.

If you're not in contact with a brujo yet, starting with Papa Legba, Belie Belcan, or Baron de Cementerio. Other than these, you can slowly add Misterios—but very carefully. Don't add Misterios to your altar just because you have an interest in them, you are drawn to them, etc. The Misterios choose you; you don't choose your Misterios. Many problems can come as a result and usually do. When you do this, it can be difficult to trace back where the problems are coming from.

At one time, a woman had started a small group of people to serve the Misterios in her area. She had been initiated and undergone great changes and blessings in her life and had experienced many miracles from having her initiation. So she thought that she would like to share that with others. Not totally understanding the spiritual world nor the Misterios, and not getting proper guidance from her teacher and Papa, she started the group. She began encouraging people to set up altars and serve the Misterios on their own. At first, people were amazed at the magic, miracles, and synchronicity they experienced as a result. But shortly they all began to experience strange problems and troubles. Nonetheless, none of them traced it back to the altars and spiritual things they were doing. The woman, too, was undergoing problems but couldn't comprehend why. In her world, she was taking care of her spiritual things appropriately. So what happened?

Finally, really ready to receive her teacher's guidance, she listened with an open ear and heart. By instructing and leading those individuals, she had created a responsibility to help them on the path. By teaching what she thought "anyone could do," she had led them into more troubles than good by not realizing how the spiritual world and the Misterios work. Many of those individuals also didn't properly care for the Misterios after beginning to receive their attention. After having received blessings, many didn't continue to take care of the Misterios and allowed things to be as a hobby, taken lightly, or when it fancied them. As such many of these altars were not properly kept. So under the guidance of her Papa, she instructed everyone in the proper dismantling of the altars. Everyone but one person did so, and they all reported a change in their luck for the better, finding things coming to normal and sudden resolutions to strange problems. The individual who didn't take down the altar ended up in an accident followed by several severe illnesses as well as problems in her family. Believing herself more capable than she was had led her to her very own pit of troubles.

Once your altar is set up, you can begin to use it. Typically, a household altar only is used to give offerings of flowers, candles, and water. Larger offerings and servicios are made through the brujo at his altar, as he will know what to give, why, and when. Incense can also be given at the household altar. Flowers are offered in the sacred colors of the Misterio they are being given to: Metresili pink, San Miguel red, Anaisa yellow, Papa Legba white, and so on. Likewise, white candles are given or candles in the colors of the Misterios they are being given to.

To use the altar, you light a white candle and pray to God first. Being Catholic in background, most servidores pray three Our Fathers, three Hail Marys, and three Glory Bes. Speak with Papa Legba, asking that the gate be opened between you and the Misterios. You can then make the prayer to the Catholic saint of the Misterio you are going to offer to. Light the candle that you will give to the Misterio using the white candle. Then after, you begin calling upon and speaking with the Misterio that you are offering to—talking with him or her from your heart. Tell the Misterio that you are offering the candle, and if you are offering flowers make that known as well. You should speak with the Misterio as if he or she were standing before you. You can allow the offering candle to consume itself. The white candle you can shut off and use as an altar candle.

Flowers should be removed once they have dried up. Incense can be of any kind—sticks, cones, or resin-based. Ashes can simply be thrown away as well as candle wax remains. It's important to keep the altar neat and clean. Keeping one is a responsibility. In fact, it's better to have no altar at all than to not properly care for it.

You can also pray at your altar daily, morning and evening. In such cases, simply light your candle. Pray to God first, then pray and talk with your Misterios. It's about building the connection. You should start to look out for and pay attention to your dreams. Also look for signs coming from the Misterios in your daily waking life. If you are making contact, you will definitely know it.

What If I Live Far from Practicing Communities?

Spiritual work is not bound by time and space. This means that much of what you may need can be done by a brujo, if he knows how from a distance. In fact, I work with clients all over the world and have a huge international following, many of whom I work for spiritually no matter where they are living.

However, certain ceremonies and rituals throughout the process of your growth and spiritual development will require you to be physically present. The environment of magic and power helps to bring forward the same. Establishing connections with the proper Papa is needed in order to be linked into the sacred lines of power. There is nothing comparable to being with a brujo that has the power running throughout him or her. Maintaining a strong and healthy relationship with one's brujo is important, especially if one lives far away. Either way, you should still be training and unraveling your spiritual gifts. I have initiate students and apprentices all over the world and have special ways to train and develop people no matter where they are living.

Glossary

agua dulce: sweet water; name of the Division of Indian Spirits in 21 Divisions

amarre: binding spell

aplasa: assistant to the brujo/a

aplasamiento: the second initiation into the 21 Divisions

Arawak/Arawaks: a native people of the Caribbean Islands

avista clara: "clear-eyed," meaning to consult with the Misterios without being mounted

badji: altar room

baji: altar room

baka: evil spirit with limited powers

bautizado/a: someone who has undergone the highest initiation in the 21 Divisions

bautizo: lit. "baptism"; the last major initiation into the 21 Divisions

bayi: altar room

Black Division: group of Misterios that rule over Death and the cemetery

black magic: use of spiritual energy to harm or hurt; using spiritual energy at someone else's expense

Blue Division (Water): group of water Misterios

Bokos: African based term for male priest who is mouthpiece of the spirits

botanicas: a store selling herbal and other traditional remedies

Brujeria: witchcraft

brujo/a: literally "witch"; a priest of the 21 Divisions

caballo: literally "horse"; one who takes on a Misterio or is mounted in trance possession

cacique: Taino chief

callate: shut up

calvario: calvary

Centinela/Centinelas: Misterios that serve as messengers/sentinels for other Misterios

child/children: one whose under the guardianship of a particular Misterio

Cofradia: coed brotherhood

compadre: best friend

consulta: a consultation with the brujo to define the problem a person is having

curandero/a: healer or folk healer

curioso: literally "curious one"; a person who has curiosity about the spiritual realm

demonios: demon

devoto/a: devotee

Division Kriminal: group of Misterios with an aggressive manor

Division Marassa: group of Misterios comprised of all children

Division of Air: group of Misterios connected to the element of air and its attributes

Division of Fire: group of Misterios connected to the element of fire and its attributes

Division of Justice: group of Misterios that deal with and rule over justice

Division of Ogounes: family of Misterios composed of all warriors; family of Misterios that comes from the Yoruba people

Division of Petroses: same as Division Petro

Division of the Cemetery: group of Misterios of the Cemetery and death; see also *Black Division*

Division of the Indians: group of Misterios connected with the native Taino and Arawak people of Hispanola; see also *Sweet Water Division*

Division of the Sweet Water: group of Misterios connected with the Taino and Arawak people of Hispanola; also known as Division of Indians

Division of Warriors: group of Misterios composed of all warriors

Division Petro: group of aggressive Misterios that arose out of need during slavery

djab: demon

endulcimientos: sweetening; spells to smooth things out with couples

enpetrosao: aggressive when offended

enviaciones or enviar un Misterio: when a Misterio is sent out to work on behalf of an individual

espina: thorn

Espiritismo: Spiritism as practiced in Puerto Rico

espiritisto/a: spiritual medium

faculto: to have the faculties or abilities for

feast day: in the Catholic tradition the day to celebrate an individual saint

Fiesta de Atabales: ceremonies with special drums and singing given to the Misterios

Fiesta de Palos: drum ceremonies with dancing given to the Misterios to request or give thanks for favors

Fire Division: group of Misterios connected with the element of fire

Florida Water: alcohol-based cologne that is used in rituals and as offerings to the Misterios

fuerza: spiritual power

fula: kerchief that is an attribute of each Misterio

Gede: Spirits of the ancient dead that have been reborn and elevated to the level of Misterio

giving puntos: a special libation and salute during certain ceremonies; to give someone an initiation

godchildren: all the individuals who have been initiated or apprentice with a brujo

goddaughter: female initiate of a brujo

godfather: male priest initiator, teacher, and guide

godmother: female priestess initiator, teacher, and guide

godparent: priests/esses who have initiated someone

gracias: thanks

gran: great

hermandad: brotherhood

hijo/a: son or daughter

Hora Santa: prayer ritual offered to a Misterio or group of Misterios in order to ask for favors, give thanks, or work magic

Indian Division: same as Division of the Indians

initiate: individual who has undergone special secret rites and attained secret knowledge to connect them with their Misterios and is part of a lineage

Jarro Divisional: sacred vessel

Kriminales (pl.): reference for Division Kriminal; group of aggressive Misterios

Legba: Misterio that guards and rules over doors and gateways

Legba Division: group of Misterios that are connected to and have domain over doors, gates, and passageways

limpiezas: spiritual cleansings

lineage: an originating group of people from which an individual can trace their descent

Lineage of the San Elias: group of people tracing their descent from the group of master brujos dedicated to St. Elijah generations back

link: an item that comes from the individual to be worked on

llamando Misterios: calling the Misterios

lobo: wild

Lwa/Lwases: spirits who have been elevated by God in power and wisdom; spirits that act on behalf of God

macuto: straw bag

Madrina: godmother; a person's initiator, mentor, and teacher

Mai: slang for mother

Mama Mambo: initiated bruja of the 21 Divisions

Mambos: initiated brujas

Mani: a special food offering made of various grains accepted by all the Misterios; a ritual to honor or petition the Lwa, in which the same food offering is also given

Metres Ezili: Misterio of romantic love, luxury, and refinement

Metresa: female Misterio

Metresas Division: group of all the female Misterios

Misterio de Cabeza: literally the "Mystery of the Head"; primary and most important Misterio of each devotee; Misterio that is guardian of an individual since birth

Misterio Malos or Oscuros: bad angels or Misterios of Darkness

Misterio/Misterios or Mystery/Mysteries: elevated spirits of power created by God that are beyond total understanding or explanation

Misterios de la Luz: angels of light

mojao: wet

montado: literally "mounted"; when a Misterio takes over the body of a caballo to communicate with devotees

montao: another term for *mounted*

muerto: dead

nino/a: child

novena: a cycle of prayers lasting nine days

Ogou Division: group of Misterios that come from Nigeria

Ogou or Ogoun: name for the family of Misterios that come from Nigeria

Ogounes Division: same as Ogou Division

Padrino: godfather; initiating priest and mentor of a brujo

palo: literally "tree"

Palo drums: sacred drums used to call upon the Misterios

panuelo: kerchief that is an attribute of each Misterio

Papa Boko: initiated priest of the 21 Divisions

Petro/Petroses: Misterios that arose in Hispanola as a result of slavery

plato divisional: divisional plate; plate on which a special food offering for all the Misterios is given

potencias: powers

Priye/Prille: lit. "prayer"; ritual for the Misterios whose focus is a litany of sung prayers

promesa: promise ceremony

puntos: literally "points"; concentrated focuses of spiritual energy

puntos de trabajar: working points

Rada Division: group of Misterios that came from ancient Dahomey

refresco de cabeza: literally "refreshing the head"; the first level of initiation into the 21 Divisions

refrescos: sodas

reglas: rules and traditions

resguardos: magical protections

revocacciones: revocations, which turn a bad spell back on the sender

salves: sacred songs

Sanse: a spiritual practice from Puerto Rico that melded 21 Divisions and Puerto Rican Spiritism

Santeria: the path of following and being devoted to the saints; a Cuban spiritual tradition

santo: saint

santuario: sanctuary

seco: dry

servicio: service

servidor/a: servant

Sirena: a mystical mermaid

Soley Division: group of Misterios that have connection to the sun and celestial bodies

sosyete: society

Sweet Water Division: same as the Division of the Sweet Waters

tafia: raw rum

Taino/s: a native people of the Caribbean Islands

tcha tcha: sacred rattle used by the brujos in the lineage of the same name

Tierra Caliente: literally "Hot Land"; referring to the island of Hispanola

tinaja: a clay pot of water used when working with Taino Misterios

tonta: dummy

Toro: literally "bull"; a family of Misterios that are associated and connected to bulls

trabajar: work magic

trabajos, or trabajos espirituales: literally "spiritual work"; magic spell

tres manos: three hands

unravel: the process of developing one's spiritual power

velada: candle-burning ritual that is done to serve the Misterios

viejo: literally "old man"; term of endearment for older male Misterios

Vodou: original name for Voodoo in Africa; in Africa, Vodou was the word for spirit

Vodoun: same as Vodou

Voodoo: how Vodou was renamed in the New World by the colonizers

vueltas: literally "turns"; referring to paths or different manifestations of a Misterio; specifically used to refer to the manifestations of Anaisa

wanga: magical spell

Water Division: group of Misterios connected to the element of water

White Division: group of Misterios coming from ancient Dahomey; Misterios that are cool, sweet, and ancestral in nature

About the Author

Papa Hector is a brujo, Papa Boko, and Caballo de Misterios of the 21 Divisions and Sanse. He was born, raised, and initiated in a family lineage of brujos that practiced 21 Divisions, Sanse, and Puerto Rican Espiritismo. Since 1989, he began his path as a brujo and spiritual worker. In 2003, Papa Hector travel to Haiti and was initiated into Haitian Vodou as Houngan Asogwe, a high priest.

Papa Hector helps countless clients worldwide to resolve all sorts of issues, from love and relationships, court and legal issues, money and work problems to spiritual connection and development of power. He has performed thousands of ceremonies, rituals, healings, and initiations in the United States and worldwide.

He leads an international spiritual temple dedicated to the Misterios, with dozens of initiates, apprentices, and students worldwide. As a spiritual teacher, he offers the most in-depth training programs in Sanse, the 21 Divisions, Espiritismo, Brujeria, and spirituality online, in person, and in workshops to students around the globe.

He is the author of over half a dozen spiritual websites on the 21 Divisions, Sanse, Vodou, and spirituality, including *ezilikonnen.com, las21divisiones.com, Sansereligion.com,* and *mysticalwork.com.* His writings have been featured and used in a number of publications and articles on various forms of Voodoo. He can also be found on YouTube and hosts a Spiritual Podcast Show.

He writes a blog about the 21 Divisions, Sanse, Espiritismo, and Caribbean spirituality and its traditions at *hectorsalva.com.*

To Our Readers

Weiser Books, an imprint of Red Wheel/Weiser, publishes books across the entire spectrum of occult, esoteric, speculative, and New Age subjects. Our mission is to publish quality books that will make a difference in people's lives without advocating any one particular path or field of study. We value the integrity, originality, and depth of knowledge of our authors.

Our readers are our most important resource, and we appreciate your input, suggestions, and ideas about what you would like to see published.

Visit our website at *www.redwheelweiser.com* to learn about our upcoming books and free downloads, and be sure to go to *www.redwheelweiser.com/newsletter* to sign up for newsletters and exclusive offers.

You can also contact us at *info@rwwbooks.com* or at

Red Wheel/Weiser, LLC
65 Parker Street, Suite 7
Newburyport, MA 01950